TRUTHBUBBLE

NAVIGATING REALMS OF REALITY
AND OUR SOCIETAL SHIFT
FROM FEAR TO LOVE

ROGER KENNETH MARSH

Praise for Roger Kenneth Marsh and TruthBubble

"Roger Kenneth Marsh's paradigm-shifting suggestion that we exist in subjective realities, or 'TruthBubbles' stimulates an exhilarating journey of self-discovery that brings us face-to-face with--and helps us overcome--our fears. Not only can we expand and transform our personal TruthBubbles to best thrive in our own unique ways, but we can also better respect and appreciate the freedom of others to do the same. While this inspires the best kind of world-changing revolution from the inside out, *TruthBubble's* greatest contribution is its invitation to humanity to rise above petty fear-based limitations, toward a middle way of harmonious, balanced evolution of consciousness."

— CYNTHIA SUE LARSON, AUTHOR OF *QUANTUM JUMPS, REALITY SHIFTS,* AND *HIGH ENERGY MONEY.*

"Roger's perspective combines a clear comprehension of 'what's going on,' with a compassionate heart and a practical sense of how to make the important shifts facing us today. I love the lightness he brings with the *TruthBubble* concept as I too see us living in 'spheres' of perception. He's talking about the transformation of consciousness and we'd all be wise to listen!"

—PENNEY PEIRCE, AUTHOR OF *TRANSPARENCY, LEAP OF PERCEPTION,* AND *FREQUENCY*

"*TruthBubble* is an engaging explanation of the perceptions and conceptions you hold about your life and the world around you—from the material to the transcendent. It presents deep truths in accessible ways, offering practical techniques for self-improvement and for tapping into your higher potentials."

—JOSEPH SELBIE, AUTHOR OF *THE YUGAS* AND *THE PHYSICS OF GOD*

"With *TruthBubble*, Roger takes us on an epic journey of life from birth to death. Along the way he shows us the power of the integral approach and the importance of developing our whole selves; body, mind, heart, and soul. I have found that in life, as in sports, we can make a move towards our inner game and begin developing our interiority. Once a person embraces this path of inner transformation, and begins consciously cultivating their unique TruthBubbles, these interior changes become a game-changer and serve to transform every dimension of life. Highly recommended reading for evolutionary explorers ready to navigate into new realms of reality."

— BARRY ROBBINS, CO-FOUNDER EVOLUTIONARY SPORTS COLLECTIVE

"At the heart of this book is a message of love. With *TruthBubble*, we see that our access to whole new experiences in life, to whole new TruthBubbles, is through shifting our focus from fear to love. By courageously facing and embracing our fears, we can move through them to the other side: the side of deep love, appreciation, and gratitude for all."

— CHERYL CARLSON, LMFT

"Most of us like to believe we're free. But are we really? In the classical sense of the word, many who read this book may be. However, in the readings and reflections that lay ahead, you'll quickly discover you've been perceiving freedom through a bubble – one that simultaneously creates and limits your experience of life.

Through this book Roger is giving us a sacred moment to explore our choices and mindsets, and an opportunity for real self-inquiry on the worldviews we hold. Roger also asks us to look at how we view others and to see their TruthBubbles with new understanding and heightened compassion. In a time when buzzwords like emotional intelligence and empathy abound, Roger puts forth wisdom about what each can actually mean – with gentleness and clarity."

— JOE LARANJEIRO, PARTNER, CONSCIOUS BUSINESS INSTITUTE

"In *TruthBubble*, Roger shares his belief in the power of love and the role our heart and soul play in shaping and creating reality. He goes beyond the mind, introducing emotional, spiritual and physical exercises to help his readers cultivate their purpose, sense of truth and worldview. Get ready to feel more alive and connected to your best self."

— SHERI PATE, LMFT

"Through *TruthBubble* you will travel many miles into the world of transforming consciousness. The book pulses with positive energy and aims to dignify each person, enrich the way we see ourselves and how we hold onto our views, and encourages us to press our limits of what is possible."

— SALLY MAHÉ, CO-AUTHOR *A GREATER DEMOCRACY DAY BY DAY*
AND *BIRTH OF A GLOBAL COMMUNITY*

"Read this book! In it you will find an accessible, creative, refreshing approach to examining your Truthbubble – "the water you swim in" – and make more informed, positive choices…leading to a more peaceful, joyous and fulfilling life.

I appreciate the way Roger draws from the wisdom of the best thinkers in human potential and physics, while adding his own fresh and original ideas and examples. I highly recommend this readable book. It has permanently shifted my 'Truthbubble' for the better!"

— KIM KRISTENSON-LEE, LEADERSHIP DEVELOPMENT DIRECTOR,
LABYRINTH LEADERSHIP GROUP

"This new work from Roger, *TruthBubble*, presents a human journey from fear to love through compelling examples, a rich set of influences, and the power of heart infused with divine love. It is inspiring to absorb Roger's unwavering truth and to contemplate our own. Recommended for those ready to embark on a path of love for themselves and the world."

— PAM KRAMER, PRESIDENT, INTEGRAL TRANSFORMATIVE
PRACTICE INTERNATIONAL

First published: April 2021

ISBN: 9798738755934

Dedicated to my significant other, Cheryl, a blessing in my life and soulmate on so many levels. To my friends and family for their love, support and encouragement. And to evolutionary explorers of all kinds, in all realms. I salute your willingness and courage to risk what exists to discover what might be, bringing new possibilities alive for humanity.

An Opening

Place your hands over your heart

Bow your head toward your heart

Take three deep, slow breaths

In through the nose

Out through the mouth

Become aware of the power of your heart

Activate a feeling of appreciation and gratitude

For this moment

For your life

For the miraculous Universe inside which you exist

For the miraculous Universe which exists inside you

Breathe easy

Extend and radiate this loving energy of appreciation and gratitude out to others

ALL others

Thank you

Table Of Contents

"We do not see things as they are. We see them as we are."

— RABBI SHEMUEL BEN NACHMANI

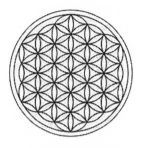

Introduction

TruthBubble: one's personal experience of reality; the beliefs, worldview or mindset that creates the world one lives inside; one's personal *truth of things* based upon their experience, often justified by collecting data and opinions of others that support it; one option of reality among an infinite number of possibilities.

What's the problem?

Some of us are in prisons. Prisons of our own mind and making. There are personal prisons, family prisons, community prisons, national prisons, all the way to global prisons for all of humanity. Many of these prisons we were put in by others as we adopted already existing belief systems and worldviews. We had to, our survival depended on it; we needed to fit in and survive in the tribe we were born into.

But as we grow up, due to the limitations they impose, these prisons cause a lot of suffering. We experience these limitations in all areas of life: health, relationships, career, and finances to name a few. There is not a single area of life that mindset, worldview, and beliefs do not affect, for better or worse. It has been said that "Context is decisive." In other words, the frame you place around something, the context you hold it in, determines what that something is for you. And, although every day we experience the effects of these frames and the prisons they create, they can be hard to see and hard to change and escape. However, with this book, your time for a jailbreak has come!

Prison is a harsh word. I've adopted the softer and more fun concept of a TruthBubble. With this book we're going to look at our TruthBubbles. We all live in various TruthBubbles, some that work for us and others that don't. It's the ones that don't work for us that we want to change.

Who is this book for?

If you're ready to create some new worlds of experience for yourself - some new TruthBubbles – this book is for you. You're probably already on a spiritual path and engaged in expanding your consciousness in some way, shape or form. If you're like me, you might be a seminar junkie: engaging this and that, looking for the secrets to the happiness and freedom in life you desire. On this journey of personal growth and development, we eventually arrive at a place where we realize "We are the ones we are looking for." We come to realize the power to change our lives resides completely within us and there is nothing outside of us we need to find or get.

Jeffrey J. Kripal, author and Professor of Philosophy and Religious Thought at Rice University said "The people who buy and read my books are typically what I call the twice fallen." For these people, the first fall is out of their family of origin. Experiencing some kind of disappointment and dissatisfaction, they set out on a journey seeking to "find what is missing." Eventually, they find a "new home" or a "new family," often in some kind of transformational, spiritual community, or some kind of teaching and process that initially provides some promise to deliver the satisfaction they are seeking. However, eventually, perhaps inevitably, the second fall comes when that new family, community or process disappoints them in some way. It's after this second fall that the person may realize, "I am the source of what I am seeking." This realization opens up a whole new world and a whole new path of exploration and discovery. I think perhaps the "twice fallen" may be the people who buy and read this book as well.

Whether you identify with the concept of twice fallen or not, this book is for you if you are ready to expand your role as the creator of your life. To stand in front of the looking glass, see what you see, and then go through it to the other side. To the side where the freedom to create your most authentic and fulfilling life resides.

Who am I and why have I written this book?

Twelve years ago I published my first book *NexGen Human – A Modern Age Path to Fulfillment*. Since then I have continued my path of transformation, growth, exploration and evolution. When I released that book, I knew I was still growing into it. The first ten chapters of the book outline the ten traits of a NexGen Human. All of these traits are infinite in their depth and breadth; when you step on the path, for each step taken two more will appear.

As I walked this path of transformation, there were many possible themes, titles, and topics I wanted to write about and share with others. Of course, I wanted to write something new and different relative to my first book. I wanted this work to be an evolution of *NexGen Human*, representing my own evolution and path of transformation. While there is some overlap in this book with my first, I came to realize that all ten traits of a *NexGen Human* add up to one extraordinary capacity; the capacity to create one's reality. This was the big "aha," the big wow, the major idea and opportunity for others I wanted to help bring into the world.

Also, in the years since releasing *NexGen Human,* the information-age has taken off like a rocket. As information exponentially increases, we are learning how difficult it can be to know what's true and what's important. This difficulty and challenge we're all facing reinforced the timeliness and importance of the TruthBubble concept.

The term "fake news" communicates the very real phenomenon of totally made-up stuff designed to manipulate people. While manipulating people is nothing new, we've gone way beyond practices of not telling the whole truth, or telling little white lies, or exaggerating things, to flat-out falsehoods widely propagated and maliciously intended for the sole purpose of disinforming and controlling others. Making things worse, well intended people pick up on fake news, and not knowing it is fake, share it with others out of their concern and desire to help. They do this usually "to avoid something bad happening," because fake news is typically fear-based and preys on human needs for safety and survival.

Add to this the internet providing a voice to *anyone* wanting to speak, the sheer quantity of messages has exponentially expanded and the impact is very real. Think of anything and you can find something about it on the internet. Everything is there; the good, and unfortunately, the bad and the ugly. In this new world we're living in, cultivating our own sense of truth and power of discernment is essential. We must learn to keep an open mind without letting our brain fall out.

As I was swimming in this information overload, I started noticing the traits of a *NexGen Human* were serving me. Especially connecting to Source, healing wounds from my past, focusing on the good, following my heart, and staying true to my soul's purpose. All of these were enabling me to navigate my life with greater ease and confidence, and to swim in the world of overwhelming good, bad, and ugly information. Beyond that, they were enabling something truly magical and profound: an ability to shape and create my reality, in both small and large ways.

I started to see that my mindset, my worldview, the context I was bringing to my life and who I was being, was having a profound impact on how I experienced life and the outcomes I was creating. The *Path of a NexGen Human* had awakened my capacities to create reality and I began exploring the principles and practices for developing this extraordinary capacity.

In *NexGen Human*, while I was aware of our extraordinary capacity to create reality, I wasn't ready to proclaim we are absolute creators; I had suffered far too much in realities I would never have consciously created. And even now, while I am to a large extent making that claim, I recognize it is a complex arena of life with myriad factors and influences at work. It's way beyond the simple approach presented in the famous documentary *The Secret*. This is why so many people were frustrated with *The Secret* – you don't simply think something and it appears in physical reality. In fact, they talk about that in *The Secret*, but they don't address the underlying factors as to why that is the case. Why do we get and experience things we don't consciously want, and why can't we always get what we do consciously want?

A big part of the reason is because each human is a complex assembly of energies – some creating what we consciously want and some creating what we consciously do not want. Also, while many of these factors can be seen and directly worked with, others are unseen and unconscious and therefore, harder to discern and work with. Nonetheless, I have seen and experienced my own powers of creation and those of many others. So much so, that I am called to present this extraordinary possibility of life for you here in this book.

What You Will Learn

I've done my best to summarize and lay out what I have found through my own research, experimentation and observation, what seem to be the most critical factors and keys for developing this extraordinary capacity. At the same time, it's important to recognize this book itself is a Truth-Bubble. Who am I to say how *you* create *your* reality? Well, indeed! And, as with anything in your life, I invite you to "try it on" and see what fits. See what works *for you*.

You are the authority of your life and I claim no absolute knowledge of and authority over the forces of the Universe and how they operate within a human life, especially *yours*! I am fully aware, and it's one of the premises of this book, that what is possible or true for one person may not be possible or true for another. And vice versa, what's impossible for one person may be very possible for another. We are each living in and creating our very own and unique TruthBubbles. With that said, let's take a look at what's here:

In Chapter 1 we'll distinguish "the water we swim in" and see the effects of the process of domestication. We need to know where we are before we can know where we're going.

In Chapter 2 we'll look at how we know what is true and what is not. It's very important for us to distinguish our "truth making mechanisms" so we can be aware of how we discern our own personal truths from falsehoods.

Chapter 3 takes us on an interesting journey into the myth that there is one "reality out there." We learn that reality isn't always what it seems to be and, as the myth makers, we have a lot more power than at first it may appear.

In Chapter 4 we look at why we, personally and collectively, create realities that result in suffering. We need to understand the mechanisms underlying and creating pain, suffering, and limitation before we are able to change them.

That brings us to one of my favorite chapters, Chapter 5, where we delve into the source of love. Here we learn the importance of coming from that place in us that provides access to creating beautiful worlds and experiences we love.

With a strong foundation now having been set, in Chapter 6 we learn how to see the TruthBubbles we're living in and how to shape and influence them in ways we desire.

That brings us to Chapter 7 where we explore the extent of our influence and power to shape TruthBubbles. Can we fly or move mountains? We'll look at some of the keys to do what I call "expand their edges."

If you've ever wondered why you cannot create the exact realities and TruthBubbles you desire, in Chapter 8 we'll go deeper to explore where those limitations reside and how you can transform and free yourself from them.

And, since we are living in a world with 7 billion other people, we must look at how to effectively interact with them and their multitude of TruthBubbles. People are living today in very different TruthBubbles, so in Chapter 9 we'll learn some skills needed to navigate in that world.

We'll see it's possible to both maintain our autonomy while at the same time living harmoniously in community.

In Chapter 10 we'll pop all the TruthBubbles and go beyond belief. We'll see that TruthBubbles rise and fall in something far bigger. And, that by realizing this far bigger aspect of ourselves, we can be free to create.

At the end of each chapter you'll notice I provide a list of *References and Resources* that will take you deeper and expand your exploration of that particular chapter's topic. Almost all of the references and resources could be listed under multiple chapters, I placed them where I felt they were most relevant.

Finally, at the end, I provide some examples of inspiring TruthBubbles for you to consider. If we are the creators of our lives then it makes sense to create the most beautiful and inspiring worlds we can. The Truth-Bubble examples provide new ways of seeing and being in the worlds of business, cosmology and philosophy, the future of the planet, and death and dying.

Ultimately it is my hope and intent with this book that you will experience a new degree of freedom in your life. Freedom to be yourself, to experience what you experience, to believe what you believe, and to create what you want to create. And, that you gain a new capacity to allow others that same freedom. The freedom to be who they are, experience what they experience, believe what they believe, and create what they want to create. By giving yourself *and others* this freedom, we can all truly be free. For me, this is a critical key for creating a world that works for everyone, for creating heaven on earth. This is my hope, my intent, and my dream, and I invite you to dream it with me.

Thank you for exploring this world of TruthBubbles. Let's get this party started!

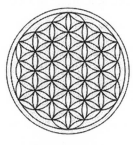

Chapter 1

The Water We Swim In

"The moment I grasped the Taoist concept of 'effortlessly following things the way they are,' I knew I had to change my whole outlook and personality."

– GREGG EISENBERG, LETTING GO IS ALL WE HAVE TO HOLD ONTO

"It's better to fail at your own life than to succeed at someone else's."

- ANDRE GIDE

Coming out of the office building of my employer around 5pm for a dinner break after already working 9 hours, I ran into another employee who said "Have a good night." I said back to her proudly with a bit of superiority in my voice "Oh, I'm not going home, I'm just taking a break for dinner and will be back for a few more hours." Without batting an eye, she replied "Suit yourself, but what I find is the more you give the more they take."

It really hit me. I didn't *want* to be working late, I wanted to be going home too, but out of some inauthentic, fear-based reason I wasn't fully conscious of, I was working long hours and becoming a resentful victim in my job. I thought, if she can claim her authority, why can't I? I was unaware of the water I was swimming in; however, this fish was waking up.

If you don't choose how you want to live, others will be more than happy to choose it for you.

Any of these sound familiar:

- Money doesn't grow on trees.
- The only thing certain is death and taxes.
- Life's a bitch and then you die.
- Money is the root of all evil.
- Keep your nose to the grindstone.
- The early bird gets the worm.
- Early to bed early to rise makes a man healthy, wealthy and wise.
- What "good little boys and girls" do and don't do.

I'm sure you can add more to this list from your own life and family. They exist in all realms of life. Notice how these make you feel. Do you feel good, relaxed, expanded, and opened? Or maybe more tense, worried, concerned, or contracted? For now, just notice and make a mental note of it.

We've all heard these sayings because they are, or were, truisms in our society. A truism is a statement that is obviously true and says nothing new or interesting. It's taken as a "fact of life," that's just how it is. We've been told things like this are true, true for everyone, no matter what. And, if you don't listen, then you contribute to your own demise.

David Hawkins, M.D., Ph.D., author and pioneering researcher in the field of consciousness, has written a series of wonderful books helping illuminate the power of our consciousness in creating our experience in the world. He describes all the various levels of consciousness and their resultant worldviews, behaviors, and experiences. In his book *Letting Go – The Pathway of Surrender* he says, "In a lower state of consciousness, the universe is seen as negative and denying, frustrating, and reluctant. It is like a bad, stingy parent. In a higher state of consciousness, our experience of the universe changes. It now becomes like a giving, loving, unconditionally approving parent who wants us to have everything we want, and it is ours for the asking. This is creating a different context. It is giving the universe a different meaning." He goes on to say "Although the world may be stingy and hostile to other people, there is no reason why we should buy into this paradigm. When we buy into it, we make it that way in our own life."

So back to our "truisms." How true are they? Perhaps they were true for someone, at some time, but does that mean they have to be true for everyone, all the time? Absolutely not! It's important to note that people who say these things are not lying and trying to deceive us, in fact they may be trying to help. However, it's even more important to notice they are telling the truth from their experience. And therein lies the key –

> We must be careful that good advice, or expert experience, does not become baggage from the past we must lug into our future. Some people may be swimming in those waters, but we don't have to.

their experience. We must be careful that good advice, or expert experience, does not become baggage from the past we must lug into our future. Some people may be swimming in those waters, but we don't have to.

Through this book we're going to learn to test beliefs, truths, and worldviews to see if they are true, for us. Whether or not they are true for others, as we'll see, doesn't really matter. What *really* matters is if they are true for us. What water do you want to swim in?

The People Influence

When we were young and growing up there were many people influencing and shaping our reality. As infants we were like sponges, absorbing everything around us as we learned about the world we were born into. Most of us probably have very little conscious memory of these early years in our lives. However, they were very formative, and to a very large extent created the "default" water we are swimming in. We watched the people around us and learned from their behaviors.

And, this perception-shaping started even before we were born! Penney Peirce in her book *Leap of Perception – The Transforming Power of Your Attention,* states "Even before the Industrial and Information Ages, brain science tells us our brains and perception were shaped by centuries of scarcity, trauma, suffering, and danger. A fairly new field called *fetal origins* studies the effects of the conditions we encounter in the womb and how our nine months of gestation may wire our brains for survival. More specifically you may be influenced from the very beginning by emotional and chemical expansions and contractions coming from your mother about whether the world is safe, abundant, loving, and creative – or if it's a place of danger and pain."

Then, as we come into this world, as a child and young adult, it's primarily our parents who are deciding how we are going to live. And that's fine, when growing up. However, for many, it continues on and on. At what point do we get to say "This is my life and I'm going to live it my way?" For some, it's never, they're always living into the expectations of the crowd, the tribe, or their parents, forever.

"We don't come to our parents, we come *through* our parents."
- T. Harv Eker

While our parents are very important and even sacred people in our lives, they don't own us. We are not possessions that they get to do whatever they want with. It's very important to understand this and break free of the good opinions of others. And, there are *many* others in our lives, no matter how well meaning, that have, and are, shaping and influencing us. Some for the better and the good, and others perhaps not for the better or good.

The process is called domestication, where we learn to function in the society into which we are born. We learn how to be a member of the tribe, and take our place, whether authentic or not. Problem is, society only sees sockets and plugs where they've always existed. They do not see the new and emerging sockets with newly emerging plugs needed for evolution of society. These are newly arriving souls that are designed to both create and plug into new sockets.

Becoming the stereotypical doctor, lawyer, or astronaut, all existing sockets and plugs, becomes the definition of success. Society has organized itself around these and thousands of other existing sockets – educational systems, economic systems, government systems - all geared to perpetuate the same old sockets and plugs. And, there's nothing wrong with this as long as you are authentically designed to plug into one of these existing sockets. But, if you're like me, and there is no existing socket to plug into, then you're on a different path, and probably need to create a new TruthBubble when it comes to vocation.

Others in our circles with tremendous influence on our beliefs and worldviews are teachers, coaches, clergy, counselors, and of course our circle of friends. I feel these people are often coming from a place of intention to help; however, they cannot see what is true beyond what is true for them; they cannot see what *you* are here to be, do, and have, especially if that is something new, unusual, or apparently to them, risky. It's rare that a person can see their own TruthBubble and own it in a way that does not inflict it on others. TruthBubbles are the water we swim in; we can't see it just like we can't see the back of our head. It's the way the world *is*, not our perspective, but rather reality itself.

> It's rare that a person can see their own TruthBubble and own it in a way that does not inflict it on others. TruthBubbles are the water we swim in; we can't see it just like we can't see the back of our head.

Much of this domestication process is grounded in survival. I mean hey, we gotta learn to take care of ourselves and be productive members of society, right? In the western world capitalism is the name of the game and everyone is in a business of some kind, whether they call it that or not. Everyone is selling some kind of service or product to receive something of value in return, usually money, so they can obtain the things they need to survive.

The Media and Marketing Influence

Let's look further at capitalism and the culture it creates. Marketing messages come at us at an alarming rate, especially now with people plugged in 24/7. We are hit with messages of *all* kinds. Some estimates I've seen say the average person is exposed to thousands of ads per day! While these messages are designed to serve a need in your life, they are also designed to *create* a need in your life; whether to be cool, happy, safe, healthy, or loved. To create that need you must believe you don't already have what it is they are promising to sell you. Hence marketing reinforces a "less than whole" mindset. You don't have everything you need, therefore you must to buy *this* so that you *then* will have what you need.

As an example, beer companies aren't selling beer, their selling good times, adventure, friendship, or believe it or not, a slim body! The truth is, what you get when you buy a beer, is an alcoholic beverage. You will not get these other things which probably are the things you actually want. This hypnotic, manipulative engagement of our minds puts us on a treadmill of buying that never ends.

I personally feel the pharmaceutical ads are some of the worst since they may be creating a sickness or health problem you never even thought of, but now you think you might have it! And of course, they have the pill that will fix your problem, as long as you take it forever.

And how about those TruthBubbles presented to us through the news as "the facts" without bias or opinion? It's ridiculous! The selection of topics itself is a bias! I've heard CNN called the Crisis News Network. What fear-based crisis can we have people worried about today? We've all heard the old saying "if it bleeds it leads" – this marketing strategy takes advantage

We can't do something about everything, and everything is what television and the internet is bringing to us today

of our fear-based ego trying to keep us alive and watch out for problems in the world, something that is out to get us, or might get us. We are on alert. Problem is, much of the fear-based, bloody news is not something we can do anything about! Yes, there are many things we can do something about. But we can't do something about everything, and everything is what television and the internet is bringing to us today.

And of course, we have our internet-based social networks influencing and creating TruthBubbles of all kinds shaping the water we swim in. As a fish in these waters, we must be careful to not take the bait.

The Cultural Influence

It all adds up to the culture we live in. It's a huge TruthBubble and we are like the fish that cannot see the water it's swimming in. If you travel to other countries you can see how different cultures live in different Truth-Bubbles. Culture is a TruthBubble and it's important to distinguish the one(s) you are in by default. I'm an American. I'm a native Californian, Northern California mind you, who grew up in Livermore. These are all TruthBubbles. They all shape who and what I am. Just like your origins and place of living shape who and what you are.

The Bottom Line

We all have lots of automatic, default TruthBubbles we are living in. Some are good and helpful, others are not so good and helpful, even if they once were. The first step on this journey is recognizing the existence and sources of these TruthBubbles we're living in, and realizing it is the water we are swimming in. With this realization we can begin to question our TruthBubbles and empower ourselves to begin choosing and creating new and better ones.

Our next step on this journey will be to explore a question that very few of us ever ask: How do we know what is true? Let's go there now.

References and Resources

- *Reflect*: What were the most influential experiences of your life, positive and/or negative? What people, places and events have shaped who you are and how you see your world?

- *Read*: **Letting Go: The Pathway of Surrender, David R. Hawkins, 2012**

  "*Letting Go* describes a simple and effective means by which to let go of the obstacles to Enlightenment and become free of negativity. During the many decades of the author's clinical psychiatric practice, the primary aim was to seek the most effective ways to relieve human suffering in its many forms. The inner mechanism of surrender was found to be of great practical benefit and is described in this book."

- *Read*: **Leap of Perception: The Transforming Power of Your Attention, Penney Peirce, 2013**

  "As the vibration of the world continues to accelerate, we are being catalyzed into a new kind of knowing – literally, a transformative leap of perception. We can now clearly see how perception itself creates the world and our life experience. We are rapidly outgrowing 'old perception' and are discovering a high-vibrational 'new perception' that creates a high-frequency world – one in which oneness, compassion, service, joy, and mutually sourced cocreativity prevail."

- *Watch*: **From Domestication to Transformation, Transcendence Season 2 Episode 1, Gaia Original Series, 2020**

  "Uncover the true impact of our modern-day evolution on our mental health and wellbeing, and how we've been influenced by outdated systems of education and governance."

Chapter 2

The Source of Truth

"I like to learn from everybody, especially
people that agree with me."

"I now only trust the opinions of people who admit they probably
don't know what the hell is going on."

– GREGG EISENBERG, LETTING GO IS ALL WE HAVE TO HOLD ONTO

How do you know what is true? Have you ever thought about that? What are your metrics, or measures, or ways that you know what is true, either for yourself or the world at large? This is a profound and important question, especially today. We must discern how we know what is true so we can sort out truth from falsehood. If we do not know how we know what is true, we can be easily manipulated and sold all kinds of things.

A Concentric Circles Framework for Determining What's True

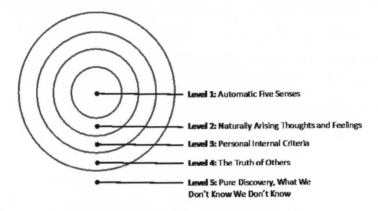

Level 1: Automatic Five Senses

Level 2: Naturally Arising Thoughts and Feelings

Level 3: Personal Internal Criteria

Level 4: The Truth of Others

Level 5: Pure Discovery, What We Don't Know We Don't Know

Level 1: Automatic Five Senses

As shown above, an easy framework to approach this question is to think of concentric circles. At the center is a circle representing you and all of your senses. Let's start with the basic five senses of seeing, hearing, smelling, tasting and touching. As we interact with the world around us, we use these five senses to determine what is true. For example, do you like broccoli? Well, to find out you'll do a little experiment; you'll look at it, you'll smell it, and you'll taste it to determine yes or no; I do or do not like broccoli. Of course, whether you like it or not could *depend* on lots of things. Was the broccoli fresh? Was it raw or cooked? Did it have a sauce, a dip, or a cheese or some kind of seasoning on it? All these factors matter with respect to your truth about whether you like broccoli or not. This may seem pedantic; however, it is very relevant for determining our basis for discerning what is true for us.

We look at, smell, and taste the broccoli to determine if we like it or not. We determine what's true for us. Notice that if we taste it and we do not like it, why is that? What has determined that we do not like it? Is that something out of our control? Can you make yourself like broccoli? Most of us would say no. Why not? Well, we say, we just don't like it. It's not "good" on our palate, or to our sight, or to our smell. Yes, but *why* is that? Where do those preferences, those *personal truths*, come from?

Some people will like broccoli, regardless of how it is prepared, and others will not like it. We can see this clearly right? We can see that we have innate, very unique, very personal preferences for what is true for us. It's easy to see this with food preferences. Look at the wide world of food that is available to us. You have patterns for eating that are unique to you. It's probably true that no one eats and drinks the same things in the same way you do. We are utterly unique! If you live with someone, notice how what they eat and drink is different from you. There may be overlap, of course, but yet, even in the same household there are unique preferences.

My girlfriend hates almost all seafood, it is disgusting to her. I love it! Where does her "hating of seafood" come from? Sometimes we can see trauma in the past. For example, when I was four years old a neighbor gave me a bite of his sandwich that had a lot of mayonnaise on it. It tasted really gross to my 4-year-old mouth. I did not like mayonnaise for a long time due to that experience. However, at some point along the way, I tasted it again and I liked it. So, my preferences had changed. Did I change them? How did that change happen? Where do these preferences come from and what is their source of change?

Now back to the concentric circles model, with you at the center, where we use our five senses to determine what's true for us. This is very clear in the world of foods. It's also clear that while there is certainly overlap in food preferences among people, there are also differences in food preferences. Just because you like broccoli, it would be ridiculous to insist, or even believe, that everyone must like broccoli, or does like broccoli, or even more crazy that it's *right* to like broccoli and *wrong* to not like broccoli.

> **Just because you like broccoli, it would be ridiculous to insist, or even believe, that everyone must like broccoli, or does like broccoli, or even more crazy that it's *right* to like broccoli and *wrong* to not like broccoli.**

We innately understand that different TruthBubbles, different experiences, realities, and therefore truths, exist in the world of food preferences and we are OK with that. While I *wish* my girlfriend liked seafood, there is nothing I can do to change that TruthBubble for her. Believe me, I have tried many times by giving her what I thought was wonderful, even the best, seafood. For example, I love a perfectly seared Chilean sea bass, where it is golden brown and bit crunchy on the outside, but super tender and moist and flaky on the inside, usually with a butter, garlic and white wine sauce, and no "fishiness" about it. She will taste what to me is an amazing piece of fish and say that it is too fishy, or gross. It's just not in her TruthBubble and I can't put it there.

Level 2: Naturally Arising Thoughts and Feelings

So here we are in the center of our circle, of our TruthBubble, with our five senses determining what's true for us. This is easy to see with food. Let's now ramp it up and move outside ourselves to something a bit more removed. Let's use movies. What kind of movies do you like? I like comedies. I love spiritual documentaries. I like heartwarming, uplifting, positive, educational movies or documentaries where I learn something and feel good and inspired after watching them. Notice I am using my feelings as a measure of what I like, what is true for me when it comes to movies and documentaries. To determine what's true for us in this more "removed from us experience," we must pay attention to our more *internal* states, our thoughts and feelings. In other words, what does it make us think and feel?

In addition to what we see and what we hear, we use our internal barometers of thoughts and feelings to determine our preferences for a movie and whether we like it or not. We do not taste, smell, or touch in a tactile way a movie, so we must use these additional sensorial tools of thoughts and feelings to determine what's true. I do not like horror movies – they encourage in me fear-based thoughts and fear-based feelings. I do not enjoy being uncomfortable like that. However, obviously, many other people do. Many movies on TV are horror films. Most of what Hollywood is producing is fear-based and evokes feelings of fear for people. These movies are very successful, people pay to see them, and Hollywood makes money on them. It is not my TruthBubble, but it is for others.

So why do some people like horror films and others, like me, hate them? Where do these preferences, these truths, come from? What's true for me is I hate horror films. What's true for others is they like them – they like being scared, feeling fear, thinking scary thoughts. They like it, I don't. Clearly there are differences in experience. Same movie, same broccoli, different experiences, different *truths*.

Level 3: Personal Internal Criteria

Here's another example, perhaps a bit more removed from our direct experience than a documentary or movie – beauty. What is beautiful and what is ugly? There's a reason we say beauty is in the eye of the beholder. This says that the truth of beauty is not "out there" but rather "in here," in the beholder. This is another great example of how a truth does not actually exist out there in the supposedly "real world" or reality. Yes, there may be some common experiences of beauty. Someone may look at a sunset over the Pacific Ocean, experience it as beautiful, and say to the person sitting next to them looking at the same sunset and ocean "That is so beautiful." And this person next to them may agree and say "Yes, it is." However, they are actually not experiencing the same sunset. It is being filtered through two totally different sensorial mechanisms. Yes, as two *human* sensorial mechanisms there are some overlaps, however there are far less overlaps than what we might assume.

How about our determination as to whether something is good or bad? How do we determine "the truth" of something being good or being bad? What are our measures for determining this? Those measures could vary widely from person to person, and they might change based on prevailing circumstances.

Here's an old story illuminating how our determination of good luck or bad luck can depend on the circumstances within which it occurs; both those in the present and those in the *unknown future*. A farmer had a beloved horse that got out of the corral and ran away. Well, you might say, that is bad, or even bad luck, he lost his beloved horse. The next day that horse comes back followed by another horse. Now the farmer has two horses, wow, that is good, or good luck. This second horse is a wild horse and needs training, so the farmer's son tries to break-in the horse and while doing so is bucked off and breaks his leg. Oh no, now you might say the arrival of the new horse, that *was* good luck, is now bad luck since the farmer's son can no longer do any work on the farm.

A couple days later there is knock on the farm house door. The farmer opens the door and sees military officials who are going door to door conscripting young men to go to war. The farmer's son would've been taken to war, however since his leg was broken, he was not taken. So, is something good luck, or bad luck? Looks like it depends.

As we move out in our concentric circles model, we find it becoming more and more difficult to determine what's true for us. This is because our ability to directly experience something becomes less available, e.g., we can't taste a movie. We find we must rely more and more on personal internal criteria, many of which are not consciously chosen and are therefore unconsciously operating. And, because we cannot know the future, what's true, as we saw in the example with the farmer, is dynamic and *relative*. Relative to changing circumstances within which our truth is determined. So, as we can see, it's getting harder and harder to know and say what's true as we expand out and our experiences become less and less intimate and personal.

Level 4: The Truth of Others

Let's now expand the concentric circles even further. Out to something you cannot easily have a direct firsthand experience with like you can with broccoli, or with a movie, or with a sunset. For many, extraterrestrials, spirits and angels will fall nicely into this category. If you have directly experienced any of these, then you likely relied on the senses we've already covered to determine how true for you the experience was. Many people who have experiences of this kind report "it was as real, or even more real, than my experience sitting here talking to you right now." Having that kind of personal experience tends to create a truth for that person, and would do so for any of us.

But let's say you have not directly experienced E.T.s, spirits or angels. In this case we must rely on the reports of others as to whether they actually exist or not. Just because I have not experienced them, does not mean they do not exist in the Universe. It's true they do not exist for *me*, however, as we have seen, that does not mean they do not exist *for everyone*. So, in this case, I must rely on the reports of others, their sensorial experiences reported to me second hand. The more expert, credible, and non-biased I believe these people to be, the more I can believe them and adopt a position that E.T.s, spirits and angels do in fact exist and they are real in some way, shape, or form. They exist personally for some, directly in their TruthBubble, and indirectly for me. They are included in my TruthBubble, but only indirectly through the reports and experiences of others that I trust to be telling the truth.

This is how we can expand our TruthBubbles to contain experiences or realities that we ourselves cannot or have not directly experienced. We do this A LOT. In fact, most of our realities are determined this way. For example, how do you know how far away the sun is from planet earth? Others may have told you it is approximately 95.5 million miles away, and you believed them. However, you probably have not measured it yourself, with equipment and a process you understood to be reliable, to absolutely know how many miles from earth the sun is. To make matters even more challenging, I got that number from a Google search. Do I trust Google to provide me accurate facts, from "trustworthy" sources? Do you? We're on a slippery slope here ☺

In addition to the perceived credibility of the source of information, the larger the number of people saying something is true the more we allow ourselves to believe it. We can call this consensus reality. If one person says something is true, well maybe

> If one person says something is true, well maybe it is, but if thousands say something is true, then we tend to believe it.

it is, but if thousands say something is true, then we tend to believe it. Even though it may not be true, or doesn't have to be true for us! This has been called group think, or worse mob mentality, but call it what you will, it is one way we use to determine truth from falsehood.

Let's look at another example in this far out circle in our model that is a bit closer in than the distance to the sun. Consider Jeena, someone you've never met, but lots of people you know have met her. All these people you know that have met her say she is insensitive and uncaring. But is it *true* that Jeena is insensitive and uncaring? Well, if one person says this about her that's one thing, but if lots of people say this about her, you will more than likely think it is true about Jeena, even though you've never met her. You might say, "I would wait to determine it until I've met her." Great, you're starting to get how this works! But even so, your "filter" as a human being has been influenced by these truths of others, such that when you actually meet Jeena, you'll be sorting her behaviors to see if there is any "evidence" from your perspective and in your experience, as to whether she actually is insensitive and uncaring.

Level 5: Pure Discovery

Sometimes we discover what's true for us, or possible for us, by accident. Like the time I tried to quit my job. I'd had it; another job that sucked the life out of me. I'd given all I could and it was never enough. I was miserable. It had been a long time coming and today was the day, I was going to quit. The job I needed so badly only 2 years earlier and was so relieved to get, was now the biggest burden and nightmare of my life. On my 45-minute commute I practiced how I was going to break it to my boss. I was mad, I was fed up, and I was ready to go. Then BOOM! I got a flat tire. What the? Now I'm gonna be late. I'm gonna get dirty and this whole thing sucks!

While I'm on the side of the road changing the tire my phone rings. It's one of my friends. I don't even remember why he was calling me at 8:30 in the morning. I tell him I'm changing my tire and am on my way to put in my 2-week notice and quit my job, I'm so sick of having no life and working my ass off. He says, oh, OK, but just keep the door open to do some part-time work or consulting. This was something I had never done before and had never considered. My TruthBubble around work was full time or nothing. At first, I hated this idea. I wanted free of this job and company and wanted nothing more to do with it. But, somehow, his suggestion stuck with me.

During the extra time it took to get my tire fixed my emotions cooled off a bit. And, as I drove the final 15 minutes to my office, cooler heads started to prevail. Taking a deep breath, I went in to see my boss and announced my 2-week notice. He was shocked, had no idea this was coming, and was worried since there was so much work to be done. Seeing the panic on his face I said I would be willing to work part time, but on my own terms. He said, great, put what you need in a memo and send it to me as soon as you can. I put exactly what I wanted into that memo — my hourly rate, no more than 20 hours per week, working from home, coming into the office only when absolutely necessary, and the projects I was willing to work on. I got it all, and in that moment launched my corporate consulting practice.

In my original TruthBubble the only option to working full time was not working at all. But by accident, almost literally, I discovered I had other options I wasn't aware of. My TruthBubble expanded and now included more.

What about the Scientific Method?

Yeah! What about the scientific method? Where does that fit in with respect to how we know what is true? It's a great question and we're going to talk more about that in our next chapter. However, for now, let's just say there is nothing any human can do that isn't filtered through their direct, personal experience. There is no escaping your own "truth making mechanisms." You can't get outside them. As Jon Kabat-Zinn said with his great book title, "wherever you go, there you are." Everything you say is true for you must come to you through these concentric circles. And while we may say science is looking objectively at an objective world "outside of us" and "determining what is true," we'll see that is not the case.

The Bottom Line

We have these concentric TruthBubbles from the very personal, directly experienced and validated truths to further and further out from us realities where we need the experience and belief systems of others to help us ascertain what is true for us. All the way out to the literal *discovery* of worlds and possibilities that *can* be true for us, but were previously unknown.

Now having a sense of how we know and determine what is true for us, the next question is, where do you draw the line on what is true and what is not? Let's go a bit deeper down the rabbit hole and explore the myth of a "reality out there."

Chapter 3

The Myth of a Reality Out There

"The truths of today are the myths of tomorrow"

- Edgar Mitchell, Apollo 14 Astronaut, Founder
Institute of Noetic Sciences

"All truth passes through three stages. First, it is ridiculed. Second, it is violently opposed. Third, it is accepted as being self- evident."

- Arthur Schopenhauer

I love beaches, and one of my favorites is at the Santa Cruz Beach Boardwalk in California. It has the amazing combo of an amusement park with a world class California beach. For my birthday one year my girlfriend and I stayed at a hotel right on the beach with a view of the Pacific Ocean, it was great. When we checked into the hotel, they made it very clear there were NO late checkouts. There were even several signs in the room saying the same, that checkout was 11am, no late checkouts were allowed. You would be billed an extra day if not checked out by 11.

After our two-night stay, when it came time for us to leave, we were not ready at 11am. We finally rolled out of the room around noon. The last hour of our time in the room was colored by this impending late checkout fee. My girlfriend was convinced we were going to get in trouble and have to pay the extra fee and kept telling me to call down to the desk to let them know we'd be late. I felt that would just draw attention and energy to the situation, so I chose to remain calm and affirm that everything would be fine and there would be no extra charges.

No other hotel in my entire life had ever charged me for late checkout, and while this one was unique in its very clear policy of no late checkouts, I felt confident in my position we were doing no harm – it wasn't like the maids were waiting outside the room to clean it, or that someone else, in a hotel of probably 100 rooms, was urgently in need of it. Meanwhile, my girlfriend was convinced we'd have to pay.

As we went to the lobby to checkout, we took our place in line. While standing there, we overheard the conversation between the desk agent and the guest checking out in front of us, also apparently late. We overheard an argument where he was being charged for his late checkout and he was irritated by this fee. My girlfriend elbowed me in the ribs and gave me that look that clearly communicated "See!" I must admit, my confidence was now wavering, but I maintained a cool head, cheerfully affirmed to myself that checkout would go smooth and there would be no extra charges. And if there was, fine, I'm not going to resist it, we certainly were warned.

It was finally our turn. "How was your stay Mr. Marsh?" "Oh, it was excellent, we love this hotel, the location is perfect, everything was wonderful." "I'm glad to hear that Mr. Marsh. Should I keep the charges on the credit card you provided at check-in?" "Yes, that would be fine."

"Would you like a copy of your receipt printed?" "Yes, please, I would appreciate that." "Here you are. Thanks for staying with us Mr. Marsh, we hope to see you again soon." As I turned away from the front desk, I quickly glanced at the receipt to see if there was a late check-out charge added to the bill. Nope, nothing. My girlfriend couldn't believe it, how could that be? We saw the person in front of us getting billed for it, but not us. For me it was clear, it was my power of positive thinking and creating the TruthBubble I wanted to experience. She agreed and it's been a representative miracle story for our ability to create our own realities and TruthBubbles ever since.

Who's in Control?

What is "reality out there" and who determines what it is? Looking more deeply at our example above, is it the hotel, the desk clerk, my girlfriend, me, cosmic karmic destiny, or some combination of these? What is the source? While all of these may play a role, I propose the most powerful influence, and certainly the one you have the most control over, is *you*; the one experiencing the reality, the main character in *your* movie.

We can look at this logically and discern the depth or strength of desire for a particular outcome to occur. Who had the most to lose or gain? Who has the greatest interest in reality occurring a certain way? In this example it was me. I was the one who was going to pay the fee, so I had the most interest in it. The desk clerk is an employee of the hotel, not likely totally interested in me paying one way or the other, though she did apparently charge the guest ahead of me. And the hotel, while clearly interested in getting rooms vacated on time, isn't going to miss one late fee not being charged. My girlfriend was an observer of the incident, and was not fully committed to any particular outcome. While perhaps preferring the no charge outcome, she was not committed and faithful to that outcome like I was. In her world there was a predictable reality that was going to charge me for our late departure, especially when we heard the guest in front of us being charged the late fee and arguing against it. In that moment even I, the one most committed, began to waver in my faith that a no charge reality could occur. However, I stayed strong, fully accepting the fee should it be charged, offering no resistance to the outcome whatever it may be, and continued to affirm a smooth checkout with no extra charge added for late checkout. I was committed, but not attached.

So, it is me who is most invested in a particular experience unfolding and therefore we could say I am exerting the most influence for a particular outcome *in my life* to occur. In a sense it was *my* faith that pulled it through, for me.

Synchronicity - A Matter of Meaning

This event was steeped in meaning for me and for my girlfriend. The late psychologist Carl Jung defined the term synchronicity as an acasual event in the external world which coincides with things going on in one's internal world such as thoughts and feelings. As Jung writes in his book *Synchronicity: An Acausal Connecting Principle*, "What I found were 'coincidences' which were connected so meaningfully that their 'chance' concurrence would represent a degree of improbability that would have to be expressed by an astronomical figure."

It's also important to note that an outside observer to the events will most likely say that the fact I was desiring and intending a no charge outcome, and the fact it happened, is simply a coincidence. In other words, there is no connection between my intention, or thoughts and feelings, and the events experienced in the outer world. And because of that, it is not a "meaningful" event, just a coincidence to be quickly and easily dismissed. However, for me and my girlfriend it was a deeply meaningful experience, so much so that it was a miracle that it occurred.

The Power of Intention

Here's another story illuminating the power of internal states, or what we can call intention. In the mid-1990's when I was just beginning to become aware of my inner world and its effect on the "outer" world, I was working for a Fortune 500 company as a Product Manager in the Marketing Department. This particular company had been an innovative leader in its field when it was founded, however over the years it had lost its competitive edge, and its market share and respect were both slowly dwindling. As a Product Manager, I wanted nothing more than awesome, innovative, super-competitive products to bring to my salesforce and customers. I knew I needed to reenergize the product development teams and have them find new inspiration, creativity and ingenuity.

The VP of Research and Development was one of the original co-founders of the company. He knew that a breakthrough was needed and was very open to new ideas. I approached him with the idea to put ten cross functional volunteers from the product development teams through the Landmark Forum; a three-day program that powerfully puts the past in the past and opens up future possibilities. Exactly what this company needed.

We got our ten volunteers and reserved their spots in an upcoming training. Back then the program was about $350 per person, so we received an invoice for $3,500.00. After some time, I don't remember how long, the Director of the Landmark Education Center where our participants were going to attend their program called me to say he had not received payment and asked if I could help. I told him I would go down to accounting and "check on it." In that moment he said, "Roger, rather than going down and 'checking on it' (in a passive manner), I invite you to set your intention and go down and intend that it be paid."

Frankly, this set me back on my heels a bit since it seemed aggressive. However, I had a good relationship with the Director and enough experience with the approaches taught in Landmark Education that I was able to hear his coaching and accept his invitation. I set my intention to have it paid in full asap, and went down to accounting.

As I approached the accounts payable department, I found one of the clerks and said "I'm here to check on an urgent payment that needs to be made" and told him the details. He looked around, did some typing on the computer, and then said "Ah yes, here it is. No it has not been paid." "Can you send payment for that today?" I asked. "Let me see. Yes, we can do that, no problem." "Great, thank you!"

Once again, I experienced Carl Jung's definition of synchronicity since I was certain that the setting of my internal intention as coached by the Director had made all the difference in getting that payment made asap. I knew that had I gone down there with a "how's it coming along" way of being, it would've stayed in the payment queue for who knows how long. It's clear that changing my internal state and intention led to me saying different things and taking different actions, but that's the point. My internal state affected external realities and led to different outcomes.

"Personal intention carries great power. Intention is what you consciously or unconsciously aim for or establish as purpose. Your intention, if strong enough, has an almost unbelievable power to create your reality."

- George Leonard, Leonard Energy Training Principle #8

Amazing Science and Extraordinary Experiments

You're probably familiar with the physics experiment called the double slit experiment. This is the experiment where what is observed is either a particle or a wave depending on what is being measured, depending on what the observer, or scientist is looking for. If there is a measurement taken, then the energy is a particle. If there is no measurement taken, no observation, then there is no particle and the energy occurs as a wave.

One interpretation of what this extraordinary experiment demonstrates is the power of observation itself to change what is observed. The very act of observing something, indeed expecting something, causes what is called a collapse of the wave function into a discrete particle or event. This starts to point out there is no such thing as "objective" science or study. The intention, hypotheses, or presence of the researchers is biasing the study from the very beginning. You cannot, even in so called double-blind experiments, block the effect of intention, of desire, of expectation, of one's consciousness, because as we know, wherever you go there you are; conscious intention permeates reality everywhere.

Scientist Ilya Prigogine said "Science is not done *on* nature, its done *within* nature." The myth of our being separate, above, and beyond the natural world is breaking down. Our science itself is showing us just how integrated and integral to the natural world, in fact the Universe itself, we are. In his book *The Living Universe* author Duane Elgin says, "Our Universe is participatory; there are no observers. To transform our planetary crises, we need to move past a paradigm of separation and exploitation and learn to live sustainably on the Earth, in harmony with one another, and in communion with the living universe. We are beings of cosmic connection who are learning to live in a living universe."

The double-slit physics experiment is amazing enough, however there is a more recent experiment that is even more amazing that you may not be aware of. In this experiment researchers set up two measuring devices, two observers, looking at the *same* event, and got two different results! We think that if there is an event, there is only one event, and that if two people are looking at it they will see the same thing. This experiment is suggesting that even when looking at the same event, two people can see two totally different things!

Here's the headline for this experiment in the online *MIT Technology Review*, March 12, 2019:

A quantum experiment suggests there's no such thing as objective reality

Physicists have long suspected that quantum mechanics allows two observers to experience different, conflicting realities. Now they've performed the first experiment that proves it.

Following this, in her April 2019 RealityShifters newsletter, Cynthia Sue Larson, who has a degree in physics from UC Berkeley and is the author of *Reality Shifts: When Consciousness Changes the Physical World*, reported:

"… exciting results from a quantum physics experiment that according to the *MIT Technology Review* appears to provide evidence that two people can observe the exact same event, see two different things happen, and both be correct. Physicists at Heriot-Watt University in Edinburgh succeeded in bringing a classic Gedankenexperiment (thought experiment) out of the realm of pure conjecture and into the real, physical world of a physics laboratory. The thought experiment requires two people to observe one single photon–which is a quantum, or indivisible, unit of light. Quantum particles can behave as either particles, or as waves, settling into one state or the other (particle or wave) at the precise moment it is observed. All the rest of the time when the particle is not being observed by someone, it exists in a 'superposition of states' in which it can be considered to be simultaneously both 'particle' and 'wave.' When a second person is unaware of the first person's observational measurement, this thought experiment proposes that the second person who is unaware of the first person's measurement might be able to confirm that the photon still exists in a quantum superposition (undecided) state.

Scientists including Caslav Brukner at University of Vienna in Austria and Massimiliano Proietti at Heriot-Watt University in Edinburgh took this experimental concept and created an experimental apparatus involving lasers, beam splitters, and six photons to be measured by various equipment representing the role of the two observers. Preliminary results appear to provide real evidence that within quantum physics, our assumption of shared objective reality may be inaccurate."

> Preliminary results appear to provide real evidence that within quantum physics, our assumption of shared objective reality may be inaccurate.

A Reality Out There?

Wow, as extraordinary as that is, I bet you've experienced a similar kind of result in your own life. Have you ever been in a situation where you were with one or more people and you all experienced something, but the stories of the experience or the realities of what happened were all a little, or a lot, different for each person? What did you assume about that? You probably assumed that some people were more or less present, or not really paying attention like you were. Or that you weren't really paying attention, or that others were biased in their observations wanting or expecting to see something that really was not there. Or maybe others were under the influence of alcohol, or can't see or hear very well, or a whole bunch of other reasons why the stories of what happened would be different for the different people.

While all of these things might be true, note that all these reasons are assuming there was "A reality out there," that something happened and it was the same something for all witnesses to see and experience. We assume there is a reality out there and that differences in experience are due to other factors, factors other than "there are literally different realities occurring for each person."

Reality Depends on Personal Capacities

It's understandable that we want a stable, predictable reality out there; that we want there to be the same thing happening for everyone. It scares us to think that reality may be that unreliable or unpredictable. Even though people may be experiencing different realities due to the various reasons given earlier, let's look more closely at this factor we can call "personal capacities."

Let's say someone is color blind – they do not have the personal capacity to see a particular color, let's say green. I'm sure we can agree that if people are color blind, they will see a different world than we do. But do you say that green exists, because *you* see it, and that they don't see it because they are color blind? Consider that green literally does not exist for the color-blind person. They are, in fact, living in a different reality than you are, with no green, or whatever color it is.

Let's expand this example out a bit more. Seeing the color green is a capacity for experiencing the world in a certain way, with green in it. And not seeing green, simply means you do not have that capacity for seeing green in the world. Green exists for some, and not for others. If you see green, we could say you are now like the E.T. experiencer who says E.T.'s exist because you see them. But if others do not see them, they literally do not exist for them in their reality. They are in a *different* reality. The reason we say green "is a reality out there" and that some people are just color blind and can't see it, is because of the large number of people who have this capacity to see green, and who all agree that it exists. Hence, we believe it does. And, probably, even color-blind people believe it exists, even though they don't see it, because so many other people say it exists.

With Extraterrestrials, it's the opposite. The majority of people do not see them and hence the narrative defining "reality out there" for most people, is that they do not exist. And, very importantly, something is wrong, or strange, or off, with people who do see them, since we know *they actually do not exist*. We think people who see them must be hallucinating, on drugs, wanting attention, or trying to deviously manipulate others. They're

> Generally, majority rules on what is true and what is not for most people.

not to be trusted. Why? Because E.T.'s are not real. That is the reality most people have access to, and are reporting, and hence it must be the one that is true. Generally, majority rules on what is true and what is not for most people.

But, does green exist or not? And do E.T.'s exist or not? The correct answer is *it depends*. It depends on your capacity for experience, in this case for seeing. Some people have the capacity for seeing green and some do not. It exists for the former and not for the latter. Some people have the capacity for seeing E.T.'s and others do not, they exist for the former and not for the latter. This seems very black and white, however most people, and you may be one of them, will incorrectly say green is real and E.T.'s are not. Unless you are a color blind E.T. experiencer – in that case you might correctly say "E.T.s are real and green is not.....FOR ME." And it's this *for me* that is the key.

If you experience both E.T.s and the color green, you can tell others about these experiences. And maybe those who do not experience E.T.s and the color green may someday join your reality where green and/or E.T.s exist. But for now, it's a reality that exists for them only through your reports to them. And if they affirm *for you* what is true *for you*, they can say "Wow, that's cool, maybe someday I'll experience green or E.T.s, but for now, they do not exist *for me*." Clearly, something can exist for you, or for someone else, but just because it does or does not exist for you or for someone else, does not mean it does or does not actually exist in the world, as a truth, or a reality out there, for you or for them.

> Something can exist for you, or for someone else, but just because it does or does not exist for you or for someone else, does not mean it does or does not actually exist in the world, as a truth, or a reality out there, for you or for them.

A Truth for Each Person

Here's the thing, we all of course have very different sensory equipment. This point was made earlier where we explored our source of truth. We know that while there are many similarities in being human, there are at least as many differences. What and how we see, hear, taste, touch, and smell are all very different. Our thoughts and feelings are filtered through so many experiences that we cannot expect that ANY event in the world will produce the same experience or reality or "truth" for each person, there are just way too many factors filtering reality for each person that the fact we *do* believe there is "one reality" or world "out there" is amazing!

So why do we believe there is one reality out there, one truth, or one world? Well, because we test our experiences with others. The quote from Gregg Eisenberg, "I love learning from everybody, especially those that agree with me," is relevant here. It's called confirmation bias – we find what we are looking for. As we saw with the color green and E.T. examples, we create consensus-based realities by discussing with others; by sharing with others *our* experience of reality and seeing if they see and experience it the same way. If they do, then we say we are "right" and reality *is* that way, since at least one other person sees it that way, or even eventually 1,000's. The more people that see and experience reality *our* way the more certain we are that it *is* that way, and the more righteous we may become. Since, if others don't see and experience the world in the way that it obviously *is*, there must be something wrong with them. They are not informed, they are poorly educated, or worse they are against us or out to get us.

Let's look at some more commonly experienced, simple examples where we can easily see there's no reality or truth out there. Is math hard or easy? Is basketball hard or easy? Is making money hard or easy? Is painting hard or easy? Your answer to these questions will of course depend. It depends on a lot of factors. Let's start with the first one - there is no truth that math is hard. While many people may believe this, since it tends to be the more difficult subject in school for many people, there is no truth out there that math is hard. It's not hard for *all* people. Many people find math easy and enjoyable. So, while it may be true for some, or even many people, it's not an absolute truth that "math is hard." That statement, or reality, does not exist in the world as an absolute. It's a *relative* truth, relative to the person stating it.

Let's look at the next one. Is basketball hard or easy? Again, it depends. There is no "truth" or reality out there that basketball is hard, or easy. If you are more than six feet tall, with natural athletic ability, you'll probably say it's easy, or at least fun and enjoyable, assuming you like basketball. You probably won't say it's hard like someone less than 5 feet tall with no athletic ability might say.

Notice that both of these characteristics by the way, height and athletic ability, are "god given" to a person and not something they choose or create for themselves. No one can take credit for creating their amazing height, or their amazing athletic ability. Yes, of course, athletic ability can be developed, can be trained, but if you have NO athletic ability, you probably do not like sports and are not going to play basketball in any serious way. Compared to the short person with no athletic ability, people that are tall, athletic and like a fast paced, competitive team-based game that is great exercise, basketball is at least *easier*. So, what's true? What's the reality out there? Is basketball easy or hard? It *depends* of course, it depends on the person experiencing it.

Let's look at our next example; making money. Many people would probably agree that making money is hard. Many people would say they would like more money than they have. Look at the millions of people that play the lottery, this is the easy way to make millions, pay a dollar and win money. The probability is low, but if making money were easy, then people would not play the lottery, they would just make more easy money. So, unless you actually win the lottery, people who play the lottery would probably affirm the truth, the reality, that making money is hard, hence they need to gamble to get it. However, we all know there are people for whom making money is easy, and a lot of them are willing to teach you how to do it, for a fee of course ☺. So is making money hard or easy? Once again, it depends.

We can go down the line like this with example after example. But you get the point: there is no reality out there when it comes to personal experiences. The only way we say there is a "reality out there" is by the number of people who say it is a certain way. The more people who say it is a certain way, the more we say "that is the truth" and that is the reality out there. However, for all

> There is no reality out there when it comes to personal experiences.

the people who say reality is a certain way, you can always find someone for whom that is not true, someone who is living in a different reality, living a different truth.

Let's look at some of the more "absolute truths." Take for example gravity. Does gravity exist? Is it real? Does it exist for you? Lots of people believe in gravity, this invisible force that attracts things to the surface of the earth below us. We were apparently born into this field and have been testing and validating it ever since. We let something go from our hand and it tends to go "down" towards the surface of the earth. We "believe" in gravity. It has been constant in my life, and I'm betting in yours too. But is it *true*? Is it a reality that everyone is subject to? Well, that depends, again.

With something like gravity where probably more than 99% of humanity agrees and believes in its existence, there are still people for whom it may exist, but they are not subject to it in ways that most people are. These people can levitate. I've never seen someone levitate. For me, this TruthBubble exists only because of reports from others. There are stories of people who have levitated throughout history. In the moments when they float off the ground, they have changed the "laws" of physics and are no longer subject to the invisible force we call gravity. Their truth, their reality, is a different one than that for others, they are literally in a different TruthBubble.

And here's an interesting observation about Saint Joseph of Cupertino, a Christian mystic and saint who lived in the 1600's who was known to levitate. If there was a crowd gathered around or near him, some people would see him float up into the sky, others would see him simply vibrating and radiating light, and others would see nothing. This points out the power of our own TruthBubbles to filter what we can see and experience. Just because someone actually *can* levitate, does not mean you will witness it. If your TruthBubble does not allow that, or perhaps wants to invalidate it, you will not see it. It's reportedly the same with UFOs. Interestingly, UFOs are also objects not bound by our "law" of gravity and a worldview we may be attached to. Whether you can see them or not, *depends* on your capacities for observing such phenomenon; not on their actual existence.

"We experience what we believe. If we don't believe that we experience what we believe, then we don't. Which still means the first statement is true."

- A COURSE IN MIRACLES

We know gravity is a relative force. That on other planets, or even on our moon, it is different. Some places stronger, other places weaker. So again, it is a relative truth – relative to the planet or moon you are on – but also relative to who you are and your relationship you've cultivated with gravity.

Even gravity, a thing we all "believe in" is not an absolute fact or truth, it's relative.

In other words, if you can levitate, you experience a different reality regarding gravity than others. So even gravity, a thing we all "believe in" is not an absolute fact or truth, it's relative.

Everything is Changing and Evolving

Rupert Sheldrake wrote a whole book on this phenomenon – that what we believe is the truth of a reality "out there," is not as true or constant or real as it is believed to be. Even the immutable laws of the universe based on our almighty science are not as immutable as they appear. When first released in the United Kingdom the book was called *The Science Delusion*. When released in the USA the title was softened to *Science Set Free*. In this book are amazing examples of how what is believed to be true, or constant and unchanging, in other words facts about reality, are actually changing and not absolute at all. As set forth in his introduction:

"Here are the ten core beliefs that most scientists take for granted:

1. Everything is essentially mechanical. Dogs, for example, are complex mechanisms, rather than living organisms with goals of their own. Even people are machines, "lumbering robots," in Richard Dawkin's vivid phrase, with brains that are like genetically programmed computers.

2. All matter is unconscious. It has no inner life or subjectivity or point of view. Even human consciousness is an illusion produced by the material activities of brains.

3. The total amount of matter and energy is always the same (with the exception of the Big Bang, when all the matter and energy of the universe suddenly appeared).

4. The laws of nature are fixed. They are the same today as they were at the beginning, and they will stay the same forever.

5. Nature is purposeless, and evolution has no goal or direction.

6. All biological inheritance is material, carried in the genetic material, DNA, and in other material structures.

7. Minds are inside heads and are nothing but the activities of brains. When you look at a tree, the image of the tree you are seeing is not "out there," where it seems to be, but inside your brain.

8. Memories are stored as material traces in brains and are wiped out at death.

9. Unexplained phenomena such as telepathy are illusory.

10. Mechanistic medicine is the only kind that really works.

Together, these beliefs make up the philosophy or ideology of materialism, whose central assumption is that everything is essentially material or physical, even minds. This belief system became dominant within science in the late nineteenth century, and is now taken for granted. Many scientists are unaware that materialism is an assumption: they simply think of it as science, or the scientific view of reality, or the scientific worldview. They are not actually taught about it, or given a chance to discuss it. They absorb it by a kind of intellectual osmosis."

I put this in here since the ten beliefs permeate our very culture and create default TruthBubbles. They determine to a very large extent the unseen "water we swim in," since so many others in our society, not just scientists, consciously and/or unconsciously believe them and therefore perpetuate them. In his book, Rupert takes each one of these assumptions, turns it into a question to be explored, and provides plenty of evidence to suggest other beliefs, worldviews, indeed TruthBubbles, are possible. In his summary for the laws of nature he says: "The idea that the 'laws of nature' are fixed while the universe evolves is an assumption left over from pre-evolutionary cosmology. The laws may themselves evolve or, rather, be more like habits." I like this distinction of habits. TruthBubbles, or "laws" of any kind, can be seen as habits, and habits can certainly be shaped.

Rupert, in part, is making a case that the world, in fact the universe, is evolving and changing, and that nothing is really constant. It's been said that change is the only constant and that permanence is an

> **Just because something is true today does not mean it will *always* be true.**

illusion. Just because something is true today does not mean it will *always* be true. We can see this in our own lives. We have been changing and growing since we got here. Much of what is true for you today is different than what was true for you as a 5-year-old.

The Source of Conflict

What I'm trying to free you up from is *attachment* to reality and truth. To reality and truth being the same day-in and day-out. To being the same for you as it is for everyone else, and being the same for everyone else as it is for you. Yes, you have a reality, you have a truth, but that reality is a very relative and personal one. And that is the case for ***all*** of us. Not knowing this is the source of much conflict.

> **Yes, you have a reality, you have a truth, but that reality is a very relative and personal one. And that is the case for *all* of us. Not knowing this is the source of much conflict.**

Let's look at this more closely and make it clearer: the *attachment* to a truth or reality out there being the way you believe or experience it is, is the source of arguments, wars, and suffering. Possibly *all* arguments, wars, and suffering. Why is this?

Well, first it's because *our* truth is threatened if *someone else* doesn't believe what we believe. Our world and how we are putting it together, basically *who we are*, is threatened if others are not seeing, believing, and putting their world together in the same way. We see that as a threat to our existence and our survival, and therefore we must either get others to agree with us, or eliminate them from our world. In other words, if others don't believe what I believe, then my truth and my reality is at risk.

The second reason, which is related to the first but slightly different, is we believe that in order for what I believe to be true, you must also believe it to be true for you. We need validation from others that they see the world the same way we do; that our reality, our truth is true for them too. Therefore, we are right and we are safe and we can believe the world is indeed that way. If others see and believe the same thing we do, that gives us the permission *we believe we need* to believe what we believe.

This is why *attachment* to TruthBubbles is a huge source of conflict; 1) because if others see the world differently our TruthBubble is at risk, and 2) if others see the world differently then we can't believe our own Truth-Bubble; we can't have that as a truth for us, and we really want it.

The Evolution of Truth

It is possible to grow our capacity to recognize multiple truths can be true at the same time. We now know from physics it's possible that more than one truth can exist at the same time. The truth of multiple truths being true has been validated by our almighty science. This is an *evolution* of truth — or more correctly, an evolution of our awareness of what is true.

Truth is evolving and changing *through* and as us.

As we evolve, truth evolves. The evolution of truth is the evolution of humanity; of each and every individual. What was once impossible and unreal, becomes possible and now real. As a humanity, as meaning making machines, we are now realizing there is no "one truth out there" that we must all align and agree upon in order to be safe. We are now awakening to a new truth, a new reality, that multiple truths, worldviews or experiences can be true *at the same time*. This is awakening to paradox and increasing our capacity to hold paradox. Moving beyond the either / or mindset and into the both / and. This is offering us a whole new world, a whole new peace, and a whole new possibility for our relationships with others.

> **We are now awakening to a new truth, a new reality, that multiple truths, worldviews or experiences can be true *at the same time*.**

Let's test this new possibility with an extreme example. You might say "This is a ridiculous idea. Of course there is a reality out there. Try banging your head on the wall and tell me it's not there, that the 'wall is not out there' and then we'll talk about what's real and what's not."

Well, of course the wall is there. This is not about making reality disappear. And, as we have seen, this is also not about black and white, either / or answers and solutions. This is about the both / and; reality is both there *and* not there, it's both real *and* not real.

We can clearly see that a lot of what we call truth or "reality" is due to personal filters we all have. We're all biased in so many ways, we're not all going to see and experience reality in exactly the same way. So, in this sense for sure, there is no actual "one" reality out there; there are more than 7 billion personal filters and absolutely unique experiences. Let's start there.

If 7 billion people bang their head on a wall and all say "yep, there's a wall there," that's a very strong consensus-based reality or TruthBubble. But if *one* person walks right through it and says "it's not there" what's the truth about the existence of the wall now? I would say it exists for 6,999,999,999 people, and **not** for one person. So, does the wall exist or not? Clearly, which is the case I am trying to make with TruthBubble, it depends. It depends on the person. And, as we learned earlier, for someone to witness another actually walking through a wall, the non-existence of the wall will have to be within their capacity for experience as well. So, indeed, even for the witness of the event, the non-existence of the wall exists at some level; even if they themselves cannot walk through it.

The Bottom Line - The Mistake We Make

We all look at and experience the world through our own unique filters, experiences, preferences, biases, and capacities. The mistake we tend to make is believing, or insisting, that the reality we personally experience is the one and only one that everyone does, or should, experience. It's actually only true for you, in this moment. Whether it is true for others is the beginning of one's exploration. Whether it is true at all, or needs to be, or must be, is also an opportunity for exploration, one that I am hoping this book will free you up to embrace and inspire you to explore.

In our next chapter we'll look more carefully at *why* we make this mistake and insist that others have the same worldview we have.

References and Resources

- *Reflect*: What do you think might be your biggest TruthBubbles, the mindsets or worldviews that define your experience of reality?

In what ways might this be similar and/or different from the TruthBubbles of others?

- *Read*: **Irreducible Mind – Toward a Psychology for the 21st Century, Edward F. Kelly, Emily Williams Kelly, Adam Crabtree, Alan Gauld, Michael Grosso, and Bruce Greyson, 2007.**

  "Current mainstream scientific opinion holds that all aspects of human mind and consciousness are generated by physical processes occurring in brains. The present volume demonstrates – empirically – that this reductive materialism is not only incomplete but false."

- *Read*: **Beyond Physicalism – Toward Reconciliation of Science and Spirituality, Edited by Edward F. Kelly, Adam Crabtree, and Paul Marshall, 2015.**

  "Our current net sense of the situation is that the empirical phenomena surveyed in *Irreducible Mind*, including in particular the deeply correlated phenomena of psi and mystical experience, collectively point the way to an expanded science, one that penetrates deep into territory traditionally occupied by the great world religions and that accommodates the central notion of something God-like at the heart of individual human beings and of nature itself. A pathway seems to be opening up toward some sort of fundamentally spiritual worldview that is compatible with science, one that would appeal to the large number of discontented modern persons who hunger for such a worldview but experience difficulties with scientifically problematic 'overbeliefs' associated with the traditional faiths."

- *Read*: **Beyond UFOs – The Science of Consciousness and Contact with Non Human Intelligence, Volume 1, The Dr. Edgar**

Mitchell Foundation for Research into Extraterrestrial and Extraordinary Experiences (FREE), 2018

"The historic academic research findings from *Beyond UFOs*… suggests that the physical aspects of the Unidentified Aerial Phenomena (UAP) contact experience are but a small fraction of attributes associated with this complex phenomenon. Indeed, it is the pervasive non-physicality, the parapsychological and other paranormal anomalous aspects such as OBEs, NDEs, Remote Viewing and ESP, that comprise the majority of FREE's survey responses. We firmly believe that the scientific physics, astrophysics, neuroscience and parapsychology academic community needs to take note and instead of dismissing and shunning the UAP phenomena, these fields need to embrace it."

- *Read*: **Reality Shifts – When Consciousness Changes the Physical World, Cynthia Sue Larson, 2011.**

  "Have you noticed things mysteriously move around? Keys don't stay put, wallets transport to different places, and socks go missing from the laundry. We observe reality shifts when things appear, disappear, transform or transport and when we experience changes in time. Reality shifts range from the sublime (missing socks and synchronicity) to completely astonishing (the dead seen alive again; objects appearing out of thin air; spontaneous remission; traveling far in a very short time). Learn how to live lucidly to create a life you love, positively influence the future and the past, and transform sabotage into strength. 'Cynthia Larson helps restore a sense of majesty and wonder to our everyday world. If you think science has explained away the magic of existence, you need seriously to read this book.' – Larry Dossey, M.D"

- *Engage*: **International Mandela Effect Conference (IMEC): https://IMEC.world**

  "IMEC Mission: At this time of humanity's potential Great Awakening, we, the International Mandela Effect Conference (IMEC), unite in mission to inspire, empower, and unify all curious observers. Through the evidence presented as the Mandela or Quantum Effect we bring into this phenomenon's own alignment truths which have proven themselves timeless in all religions, spiritual practices, and scientific findings. Together we Go. Together we Grow."

Chapter 4

The Source of Fear

"I suffered a great many catastrophes in my life. Most of which
never happened."

- MARK TWAIN

"The intuitive mind is a sacred gift and the rational mind is a
faithful servant. We have created a society that honors the servant
and has forgotten the gift."

- ALBERT EINSTEIN

What are you afraid of? What keeps you up at night? What runs
through your head over and over again? In my book *NexGen
Human* I write about the nature of our mind. The job of the mind, our
ego or personality, is to protect and keep us safe. The ego is created as an
illusory mechanism to help us navigate the world in a safe way and get our
needs met. That's not so bad, right? Well, it's not, until it runs amok. And,
it tends to run amok for all of us and create all kinds of suffering.

Over Reliance on the Mind

Why is this? It's because we have trained and developed our minds, our personalities, our egos, way too much. We've done this to the almost total exclusion of the many other parts of ourselves. Some people don't even know they *have* other parts. They are so identified and entrained in the mind their other parts do not even exist. This is where our fear-based way of living starts; in our minds, in the over development of and over reliance on our minds.

There is nothing wrong with developing our minds and learning how to logistically operate within the society we are born into. But that is just the very beginning; it is a baseline from which we can now grow and develop *all* aspects of ourselves. Currently, we develop our minds, and then just keep on developing our minds thinking we will "figure it all out" and that the rational, analytical mind is the end all be all for our survival and existence. Well, obviously, it's not. Almost 1 in 4 people (23%) in the United States are taking some kind of psychiatric drug

> We have a problem, and the problem is over intellectualization, over development of the analytical mind at the total exclusion of our other parts.

(Source: IQVia Total Patient Tracker (TPT) Database, Year 2020, Extracted January 2021). And almost 60% of those people are taking an antidepressant. Its startling to realize a significant percentage of our population is so depressed they're reaching for medication to survive. We have a problem, and the problem is over intellectualization, over development of the analytical mind at the total exclusion of our other parts.

Under Development of Body, Heart and Soul

The *source* of our fear is this disconnection from these other parts of ourselves, our deepest parts of ourselves. By focusing exclusively on developing the mind we have lost touch with our body, our heart, and absolutely with our soul. We have become big heads walking around on bodies. The body – which is where our heart and soul mostly reside – has been relegated to a transportation mechanism for our heads, which is mostly where our mind resides. The western culture creates brains in a jar responding to the universe thinking that is all there is. Sad.

So why do we do this? Why are we so focused on our mind and totally exclude the body, heart, and soul? Well, there are many reasons. First, it's because the other aspects of ourselves are more subtle. The act of thinking is very present. We are all very present to the thoughts in our head. And second, thinking is the process we believe produces the most impact in the world. We can think through something and then take actions from that thinking. Hence, we believe this rational, cause and effect process is the best, and even the only, way to produce desired results in the world. Feelings move so much slower and can cause discomfort whether they are sad or even happy feelings. Notice people will sometimes suppress tears of joy. Why? Because it makes them uncomfortable, even if they are tears of JOY! Feelings have been discounted in our society, especially for the masculine where feelings are a sign of weakness. We put the rational, analytical mind up on a pedestal and suppress feelings since we think that is the best way to get our needs met and survive. After all, we are smart and logical creatures.

One way I've been recollecting and reconnecting to important aspects of myself is through Integral Transformative Practice (ITP). I've been on that path as both a practitioner and teacher for more than 15 years now. ITP is an integral practice, meaning we honor and engage practices to develop our whole self: body, mind, heart and soul.

At one point along that journey, I participated in a process where, in a deeply meditative state, I asked each of those parts of me what they needed from me. Or said another way, how they were wanting to evolve. When I got to my mind it said "Stop relying on me so much, you're asking way too much of me. I'm not designed to do all the things you're asking me to do, and I'm angry and resentful about that. I'm trying to do my best with all you are asking but it's way too much and I cannot do it." Wow. That blew me away, and I knew it was true.

When I got to my heart it was saying, "Use me more, come to me more, I have so much wisdom and guidance to offer that you are not accessing and using. With me you will be able to give and experience so much more love. Use me more, come to me more." I was like, wow, that is so true.

When I got to my body, being the physical entity that it is, it had requests like more fresh vegetables and fruits, less alcohol, more fresh air and sunshine, more connection to nature, more exercise. These are all things that it loves and when given those things it can best do its job as my primary vehicle for navigating this world.

And finally, my soul was saying, "Listen to me. I am in partnership with the heart where you can hear me quite clearly. I have great guidance and inspiration to offer you, however you have to listen more deeply. Come to me and open to me and then take those actions I will offer to you. I am the rudder, the compass, and the guide for your life. I will guide you step by step, and you just need to take those steps." Again, I was like wow, yes, I know this to be true.

We all have these parts to ourselves, and they all have a place in our life, but our western culture does not understand or honor these parts. We abuse our bodies, shut down the heart, and deny that a soul even exists. Our "health" care is nothing but a band aid and has no ability to actually heal us at the core. We paste over our mental, physical, and emotional wounds, put on a smile and do the best we can. We are walking wounded in our society and we wonder why things are not working well. This leads to our anxious culture, confusion, anger, resentment, drug and alcohol addition, domestic violence, and more. What we need to get good at is healing; healing our inner children so we can drop the shields, take off the armor, and reclaim and re-connect to *all* aspects of ourselves.

The longest journey you will ever take is the 18 inches from your head to your heart.

The Hawaiian Huna tradition has a model that shows how the head, or mind, is disconnected from the universe and cannot see the big picture. In the image below you can see that while the Heart and the Hara (in Japanese hara simply means belly, at a deeper level it means one's true nature) have direct access to The Universe; the Head or Mind does not. Fortunately, this thinking aspect of ourselves has access to our Heart and Hara, and hence can receive, second hand, Universal insight and guidance. Without cultivating the connection of the

> Without cultivating the connection of the Mind to the Heart and Soul, it has no access to Universal insight and guidance, and is on its own.

Mind to the Heart and Soul, it has no access to Universal insight and guidance, and is on its own.

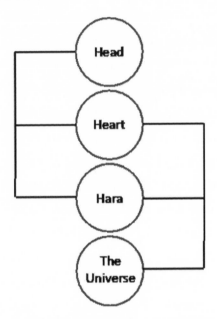

Living from the mind alone, as we do in our western culture, creates great suffering because it is not designed to be the visionary. The visionary is the connected and healed, wise heart and soul. We are given everything we need to operate and thrive in this world as long as we recognize and develop each of our essential aspects. We have the visionary soul, the loving and connected heart, the mind as an amazing manager to organize and plan, and the body as our physical implementer with its hands, legs, voice, etc.

> **Living from the mind alone, as we do in our western culture, creates great suffering because it is not designed to be the visionary.**

As I've said and I'll keep repeating, what's common in our western culture is to live in the head, or mind alone, and tell the body what to do from there. This bossy, fear-based mind is a resentful dictator. It's angry that it must be the visionary (since it cannot do it well), but it will try its best since the other options are not being pursued. Since it does not have a holistic and informed view of your life and its flow in the universe, it will scream and yell and be all kinds of anxious since it can be constantly surprised. It has to be super vigilant, and always on alert to "make sure" its plans will be successful and your needs will be met. This is very tiring, stressful, and incredibly inefficient! It's no wonder we're sick.

Penney Peirce, in her book *Leap of Perception* sheds some light on the source of this experience, "The fear-based reality to which we've resigned ourselves, to some degree was formed by our reptile brain's survival instinct and the tendency of our left brain to control reality by suppressing painful memories or knowledge that might contain disruptive emotion. Fight, flee, deny and control. A wide variety of methods for dealing with fear have developed over time from these basic tactics, then cultural worldviews grew from the tactics."

A Need for Healing

In my HeartMath® training I've learned there are two types of heart-based feelings: those that come from the emotional-heart and those that come from the wise-heart. Initially, most people are experiencing feelings from their emotional heart, which is their hurt or traumatized heart. The feelings from the emotional or hurt heart are needy, angry, and can cause behaviors that are less than productive in the world, or as Penney said, disruptive. Hence, yes, we learn to distrust our feelings, or our heart, since we are still retaining and repeating past experiences of hurt, anger, resentment, jealously, envy, etc. Therefore, we naturally shut down these uncomfortable, apparently unproductive, unhelpful feelings and go back to our head trying to "figure it out" with our rational analytical mind. What's actually needed is a process of healing.

We have hurt feelings in our heart because we have been traumatized. We were hurt as children, those feelings came up, and we didn't' know how to deal with them. Naturally, we stuffed them down and ignored them, but they don't go away. They just keep coming up when similar situations trigger us, and around and around we go. Until we slow down enough to feel those feelings, and process them in a healthy and positive way. In some circles this is called

> We have hurt feelings in our heart because we have been traumatized. We were hurt as children, those feelings came up, and we didn't' know how to deal with them.

Inner Child work. The Inner Child was hurt and didn't receive the loving mature guidance it needed at the time it was hurt, so for its survival, it stuffed those uncomfortable feelings (since it couldn't process them), and put up a shield or put on some armor, to protect itself. Until the feelings are felt and processed in a healthy and mature way, the shield is kept up and the armor is worn for protection. This is all logical and makes sense, and works at some level. But at some point, it becomes a burden.

I remember I was suffering greatly in my life, depressed, anxious, and having suicidal thoughts. Suicidal thoughts are normal when living sucks so much that being dead seems like a more attractive option. Who wants to live a life full of anxiety, depression and resignation? It's only natural to seek some kind of escape. Before committing suicide, I figured I could give therapy a try. I did some research and called the psychologist in my town that I was intuitively drawn to. In my first call with him he said something that landed very strange for me, but also somehow resonated with a truth I knew deep down inside. He said

"Roger, your mind is in WAY over its head." He knew I was trying to live my life by figuring it out, and that it just doesn't work that way. That call led to 9 months of weekly 2-hour therapy sessions that really made a huge difference in my life.

> "Don't be fooled by the large bodies and open eyes, most adults are walking-wounded on autopilot just waiting to be triggered."
>
> - DR. JOEL FRIEDMAN,

Afraid Our Needs Will Not Be Met

The anger and violence we see in the world is rooted in these fears from our childhood *that our needs will not be met* and we're understandably mad about that. Therefore, we resort to violence of all kinds; mental, emotional, and physical, in an effort to try and get our needs met. Once again, it's worth repeating, this source of fear is the belief that our needs will not be met, because they weren't at some point in our life.

Think about it, if you knew that your needs would always be met what would you have to fear? I've been engaging an affirmation for several years now that goes like this: My needs are always and forever met. That's a TruthBubble I've been consciously and intentionally creating. I've made a lot of progress and have increased my trust in life immensely.

> If you knew that your needs would always be met what would you have to fear?

We can include in "needs" ALL needs; physical, mental, emotional, and even spiritual.

You may be familiar with Abraham Maslow's Hierarchy of Needs, where human needs are stacked one on top of another in a pyramid shape.

Physiological needs are on the bottom (food, water, shelter, warmth), followed by safety (security and stability), then on top of that is belonging and love (friends, family, spouse, lover), leading to self-esteem (achievement, mastery, recognition, respect), and finally on the top is self-actualization (pursuing inner talent, creativity and fulfillment). If you knew all of these needs would always and forever be met, would you be afraid? Would you fear anything?

End of Life Anxieties

Another source of fear is our unaddressed existential anxiety about death itself. Here's another dysfunctional aspect of our western society. Just like we deny, avoid, and hide from our heart and soul, we deny, avoid, and hide from death. We pretend it doesn't exist, when of course we know that it does. This causes an unconscious yet very powerful, existential anxiety operating in our lives. Our culture is very uncomfortable talking about death. As an experiment I encourage you to try it. What I've found is that, without a lot of reflection and thinking having been done about it, people are generally very uncomfortable in that conversation. Due to the discomfort, the topic is changed pretty quickly.

After the death of my step mother, I wanted to open up the exploration of death for me and my family and friends. I thought deeply about what I believed about death and defined my TruthBubble in a piece titled "A Celebration of Death, and Life." It is included as one of the TruthBubbles at the end of this book.

In today's world there are lots of great resources to support your exploration of death. I put some of them in my article. Engaging this topic for yourself is a great way to address the underlying and unconscious fear about death and the end of your life. Until you address your fear of death, just like any other fear, it has you, it is running you, and you are not free.

Insights from Near Death Experiences

Over the years more and more people have come forward to share their experiences from being clinically dead, with no brain waves, then coming back to life. They have extraordinary experiences they remember and bring back to us. Anita Moorjani writes about her Near Death Experience (NDE) in her book *Dying to Be Me – My Journey from Cancer, to Near Death, to True Healing*. She describes a new way of seeing and being in the world after her NDE:

"I went from an outside-in view of reality to an inside-out view. That is, I used to think that the external world was real and that I had to work within its confines. This is pretty much how most people think. With this view, I gave my power to the world outside, and external events had the ability to control me – my behavior, moods, and thinking. Emotional reactions and feelings weren't considered real because they weren't tangible. They're thought to be merely reactions to external events. In that model, I was a victim of circumstances rather than the creator of my life. Even illness was an external event that just "happened" to me randomly.

However, after my NDE, I began to see myself as a divine and integral part of the greater Whole. This includes everything in the entire universe, everything that has ever existed and ever will, and it's all connected. I realized that I was at the center of this universe, and knew that we all express from our perspective, as we're each at the center of this great cosmic web."

NDE's are so informative! We get to see what's available to us beyond the ego-mind-based reality of "normal" existence, and it is extraordinary! I've briefly summarized these differences in the table below:

Heaven (NDE's)	Hell (common ego-mind-based existence)
You are loved	You're unlovable and unworthy
There is nothing to fear	You have everything to fear
You can do nothing wrong	You can do everything wrong
You're never alone	You're very alone
You never die	You're gonna die (and that's it!)

It seems "hell" is the default human experience for many of us; stuck in the mind-based orientation of existence, cut off from the deeper, more expansive aspects of who and what we are. We experience constant performance anxiety to be good enough, to be worthy, to be validated and appreciated. There is constant worry and concern to survive and we're always trying to answer the question "Am I OK?" However, through the NDE, we see there is an entirely different TruthBubble available.

Technically Connected - Spiritually Disconnected

From my perspective, the whole Silicon Valley initiative to put oneself into the Internet so you can "live forever" is rooted in this unconscious fear of death. My sense of these technically savvy people with brilliant minds is they are "thinking" their way through life, disconnected from their body, their hearts and their souls. With no experience of a reality beyond this physical world, they therefore, rightly, fear death as the end of themselves. Hence, they try to figure out ways to avoid this fear, to avoid this "end of themselves." Their solutions are expensive and frankly to me, sound like a total nightmare. Digitizing all my thoughts and feelings and putting them into a computer and trying to extend my life by living there forever (as long as there is electricity I guess) sounds like a hell if there ever was one! But to them, it seems better than what they believe, in their minds, will be the end of them – better to live in a computer than to not live at all.

Cryogenics is another one. People have literally frozen their heads (because of course that is where "they" live) so that in the future when science and technology has advanced enough, their heads can be reanimated in some way and bring themselves back to life. Attached to some kind of cyborg robot body, I guess. That again, for me, sounds like another hellish nightmare; waiting for decades or centuries, or who knows how long, in some kind of frozen suspended animation, until at some moment you are "brought back to life." "Hello, welcome to the year 2500, every relationship you ever had is dead and gone, the world is totally different than what you remember, all your memories, thoughts and feelings are completely out of sync with the new world you will now be living in, and you have no idea how to be of value, and by the way, you have no body." This is a good thing?

This fear of death is even resonating in the popular millennial saying "YOLO" – you only live once. If you only live once, then you have to do all kinds of crazy things to 1) maximize this one and only life you are living, and 2) keep that one and only life going beyond its natural end. These are the symptoms of an illness that is the result of living an existence that is only informed and experienced (if you can even call it an experience) in and through the rational mind. It's a sickness that drives all kinds of sick behaviors. And it's based in a very rational, and because of that, rationally-sourced and caused, fear of death.

Unseen and Unappreciated Miracles

Additional evidence of our isolation in intellectual jails is our complete ignorance of the miracle of life. Take for example our beating heart. It's right there in your chest. This miracle of life couldn't be closer. Yet most people have no idea how and even why it beats moment to moment. They might say "It's electrical impulses that keep the heart beating." Yes, but where do those come from? Maybe the response is "The parasympathetic and sympathetic nervous systems." OK, and what is running those? You can see that following this line of inquiry all the way to its conclusion will ultimately lead to "We don't know where it comes from or why it works." This is because ultimately, we don't know what life itself is and where it comes from. Once it's gone, it's gone.

> Additional evidence of our isolation in intellectual jails is our complete ignorance of the miracle of life.

It can't be bottled and sold, or put back in once it leaves. We can look at causes and effects, but we cannot look, ultimately, to the source of life itself. It's a mystery.

So, most of us are completely asleep to the miracle of life beating right here in our own chest. We take it totally for granted, along with trillions of other miracles taking place in the body providing the extraordinary opportunity to be here and now, awake and alive experiencing this moment. It's a miracle!

The fact this is taken for granted is another source of our fear. We are not present to the millions, in fact trillions of miraculous things happening *for* us in each and every moment. What we are is life, what we are living is life, and we have no idea what that is. It is a literal miracle. We even call it that; "the miracle of life." Yet even though we are living a total miracle, an unbelievable blessing, somehow, we're screwed. Our life is NOT a miracle. We must suffer and struggle, and complain, and be depressed, because life is hard. It is a burden, it sucks, and it's all up to little ole me to turn it out, to make it ok. Even though I can feel my heart beating *religiously* moment to moment, saying "I got you! You're all good. I'm here for you, I'm beating for you, feel me right here in your chest literally beating the drum of your life, demonstrating there is a flow, a support system, a natural harmony at work FOR you," we say "Nope, we don't see it. It's not a miracle. Nothing amazing happening here."

If we say there is nothing about life that is happening *for* us, then of course we'll be afraid, of course we will struggle, of course it will be hard, of course it will be tiring, and course we'll eventually be depressed and sick, because the miracle that we are, that life is, is going unnoticed and is not appreciated.

We are "fighting against" life by our lack of appreciation for it. We are putting our attention on how hard everything is, how much suffering there is, and how it's up to us and only us to make it turn out. Where attention goes, energy flows, and results show. Where are we putting our attention? On the miracle, on the magic, or on the suffering and on the struggle? Our heart is beating *for* us, the entire Universe is here *for* us, but we must see and appreciate it, to know it and experience it.

I know that when I am disconnected from my source of life, feeling separate and alone and that everything is up to me, then I am afraid. I'm afraid my needs will not be met, and hence I'll be suffering more and more. That is scary. That is a scary future to be living into. This fear can create anger and even violence – whether mental, emotional, or physical – both to myself and to others.

This is why our world looks the way it does – people are disconnected from their source of safety and love, and therefore are alone and afraid, which leads to behaviors to ensure survival. Often these behaviors are selfish – since if someone is concerned about *their own* survival, they don't have resources and support to share with others – it's now dog eat dog and I'm gonna get what I need for MY survival. Isn't this what we see on our planet? Yes of course there is lots of love and support being shared, but the overall, primary driver is a primal fear for survival, based in a scarcity mindset.

Hell is Other People

In 2020 the United States Department of Defense budget was $721.5 Billion dollars. This is an indicator of our consciousness, that we put that much energy into our war making machine, even if it is supposedly a "defense" budget vs. offense. The pretense being we will only fight if someone else starts it, we will "defend" ourselves. That's a lot of money, a lot of energy, and a lot of consciousness (or unconsciousness)!

This mindset is based in fear of other people and it perpetuates that fear because of its focus. Similar to the fact that the "war on anything" does not stop that thing, it perpetuates it. Mother Theresa said it best when she said "Do not invite me to an antiwar rally, I will not come. But if you invite me to a pro peace party, I'll be there." Fighting against something just keeps that same thing in place since that is where your attention is.

The art of Aikido knows this well. You don't fight *against* an attacker – like so many other martial arts do – rather you use their own energy to safely, and lovingly, disarm them, bringing them to a position where they can do no harm either to themselves or others. The underlying principle is that *they are not in their right mind* (and either are you if you think you must fight them). The fact they believe they must fight to get their needs met is the indicator they are disconnected from their source of safety and love. They have fallen to a level of consciousness where they believe they now must resort to physical violence to get their needs met. The right response to this insanity, to this disconnected person, is compassion. We must skillfully disarm the subject and begin the work to restore their connection and their experience of safety and love.

The most skillful, helpful, and appropriate response to violence is compassion. Any person resorting to violence of any kind - mental, emotional, or physical - is suffering greatly. They are afraid and they believe their needs for safety and love, for survival itself, will not be met in any other way. Have pity for these people! It's a sad and miserable state of consciousness. I know because I have been there, and you probably have too. Do not respond with more violence. As Gandhi wisely pointed out "An eye for an eye makes us both blind." Respond with love, with compassion, and invite them into higher states of consciousness where their needs for safety and love can truly be met (more on this in the next chapter).

> The most skillful, helpful, and appropriate response to violence is compassion. Any person resorting to violence of any kind - mental, emotional, or physical - is suffering greatly.

The Bottom Line

We can see we have many sources of fear and that many people on the planet are affected by these sources. However, as distinct and unique as each of these fears may appear, the bottom line and ultimate source of *all of them* is disconnection. Disconnection from body, heart, and soul.

Disconnection from the beauty of death. Disconnection from the miracle of life. And disconnection from other people. **Which all ultimately results from disconnection from the source of life itself.** This disconnection creates feelings of separation; that we are alone. Feeling separate and alone raises the fear that our needs will not be met, which then leads to all kinds of dysfunctional, survival-based behaviors. The secret is to get connected and experience and be the source of love that we all are, the topic of our next chapter.

References and Resources

- *Reflect*: What are your biggest fears and how might you better embrace, move through, and beyond them? How connected, or disconnected, are you from the source of life? How do you know or experience your level of connection/disconnection?
- *Read*: Transcend – The New Science of Self-Actualization, Scott Barry Kaufman, 2020

  "Kaufman's new hierarchy of needs provides a road map for finding fulfillment – not by *striving for money, success, happiness, or even self-actualization as a goal in itself*. Rather, transcendence emerges when we meld the best in ourselves with the best in others and the world around us. We don't have to choose either self-development or self-sacrifice; when we transcend, we experience a deep integration of both."
- *Read*: Dying to Be Me – My Journey from Cancer, to Near Death, to True Healing, Anita Moorjani, 2012

  "In this truly inspirational memoir, Anita Moorjani relates how, after fighting cancer for almost four years, her body began shutting down – overwhelmed by the malignant cells spreading throughout her system. As her organs failed, she entered into an extraordinary near-death experience where she realized her inherent worth… and the actual cause of her disease. Upon regaining consciousness, Anita found that her condition had improved so rapidly that she was released from the hospital within weeks – without a trace of cancer in her body! In Dying to Be Me, Anita freely shares all she has learned about illness, healing, fear, 'being love,' and the true magnificence of each and every human being."

- *Read*: **Surviving Death – A Journalist Investigates Evidence for an Afterlife, Leslie Kean, 2017**

"While exploring the evidence for an afterlife, I witnessed some unbelievable things that are not supposed to be possible in our material world. Yet they were unavoidably and undeniably real. Despite my initial doubt, I came to realize that there are still aspects of Nature that are neither understood nor accepted, even though their reality has profound implications for understanding the true breadth of the human psyche and its possible continuity after death."

"Based on facts and scientific studies, *Surviving Death* includes fascinating chapters by medical doctors, psychiatrists, and PhDs from four countries. As a seasoned journalist whose work transcends belief systems and ideology, Kean enriches the narrative by including her own unexpected, confounding experiences encountered while she probed the question concerning all of us: Do we survive death?"

- *Listen*: **Journey to Source – Beyond Belief Audio Program, Roger Kenneth Marsh, www.TruthBubble.com**

This program systematically frees you from the everyday cares and concerns we experience as human beings existing on this physical plane. By releasing these cares and concerns one by one, you become free to experience the very Source of your being. New insights, perspectives, and divine guidance are all available to you each time you take this journey. It has been designed with busy lives in mind and can be completed in less than 20 minutes.

Chapter 5

The Source of Love

"Love is the experience of being aligned with life-source energy."

"Tired from the pursuit of happiness, I sat down to rest,
and found that happiness caught up with me."

- ROGER KENNETH MARSH

In the last chapter we've seen we all want to be safe and loved. It's a
natural human need. However, trying to get our sense of safety and
love from other people, or trying to give it to ourselves, is incredibly
tiring and exhausting and keeps us on a treadmill. Why? Because the
problem with this approach is that the safety and love we seek and get
from "outside" ourselves, from other people and things, and that comes
from our small "s" self, is finite; it runs out. Often it only lasts for a
moment in time, then we're back on the treadmill seeking and defending
what little sense of safety and love we have and can get.

What we really need is an *infinite* source of safety and love. And, guess what, we all have it. Where is this infinite well-spring of safety and love? For me, it lives right in my heart. I can breathe into my heart and awaken my experience of infinite safety and love. I can connect to this place where everything is always and forever good, even great, no matter the external circumstances, issues or challenges. It has been called the peace that passes all understanding. In my TruthBubble, there is a place within each of us where this truth resides. And, with conscious, intentional, continuous cultivation, we can come to know this infinite source of safety and love for ourselves, in our moment to moment lives, more and more.

As we've seen, most of humanity is *up in their heads* trying to think their way through life, trying to get their deep need for safety and love met by intellectually figuring out the scheme, plan, system, approach, or strategy that will provide it to them. Most believe it will be money that gives them the safety and love they desire and that the more money they have the more safety and love they will have. We know, as many very rich people have told us, this is not true. Money is not the source of safety and love.

We see people with very little money who experience far more safety and love than almost anyone else. These people are such a mystery to us living in a western culture, how can they have so little yet be so happy, playful, and smiling all the time? Given our worldview and belief that you need lots of money to be happy, it makes no sense to us. Well, indeed, they know something we do not. They know that safety and love do not reside in material things, it does not reside in money, it resides inside oneself, and in the quality of your connections – which can only be good if you have cultivated first a healthy and positive *connection with yourself.*

We cannot think our way into the safety and love we deeply need as human beings, yet that is exactly what the western mindset has been trying to do for most of its history; the mindset of gathering as much material goods as possible in order to create and ensure the safety and love we need. Or, when it's an entire society and nation, this fear-based mindset and the behaviors it drives has resulted in the destructive empire building we've seen time and time again in many cultures. The need to go out and conquer and collect and dominate in order to ensure our safety and love has time and time again destroyed our planet and proven finite in its capacity to deliver. Whether individual lives or entire nations, this mindset and pursuit ultimately collapses under its own weight as deeper "truths" make themselves known.

> **We cannot think our way into the safety and love we deeply need as human beings, yet that is exactly what the western mindset has been trying to do for most of its history.**

We seek for our safety and love in so many places, but, as it has been said, God put it in the last place most of us will ever look; right in our own heart. So close we cannot see it; its like looking for our glasses when they are right on our head. It's the diamond we have in our pocket while we're out stressing and straining, mining and destroying the lands looking for it. It's right here closer than our breath itself.

Do you want an infinite supply of safety and love? Do you want to have an unshakable knowing, an experience of "I am always and forever safe and loved," would this be valuable to you? What would your life look like if you knew, without question, that you are always safe and always loved. That you literally have an infinite supply of love, and that you are always, no matter what, safe. How would that change your life?

We look to so many outside sources and indicators for these deeply human needs – our bank accounts, other people, the news (which of course is a terrible place to look for safety and love!), the internet, the experts, magazines, even mystics and shamans. We want and need to feel safe and loved so badly we'll do anything to get it. But what we miss in this endless search, is that its right here, already fully and freely given, ready for us to see and embrace it, in our own hearts and souls.

Now I don't want to give the impression this is easy – it may be simple, but that does not mean it is easy. For most, like me, this is a path of practice, a path of awakening, a path of development that we must consciously embark upon and continuously cultivate. Creating and knowing our absolute safety and infinite love is something that is created over time.

> This is a path of practice, a path of awakening, a path of development that we must consciously embark upon and continuously cultivate.

It's a journey we affirm and affirm, and realize and experience moment by moment. Such that, over time, we come to a place where we can say "Yes, I am infinitely safe and infinitely loved and no one, nothing, can ever take that away from me." This is the beginning of a whole new life for you, one grounded and coming from love vs. fear.

Getting Connected

One of the most important tools for your becoming and staying connected to your source of infinite safety and love, is to know the characteristics, or traits you will experience when you are connected vs. disconnected. We need to know the markers for each, especially when we are disconnected, so that we can pause and restore our connection before taking any action.

Included below is a table that outlines the traits, or you could say "what you will be experiencing" when you are disconnected vs. when you are connected. You can use these markers to assess the nature of your experience in any given moment, especially prior to taking any action in your life. When we are disconnected and operating from our small, alone and separate sense of self, our fundamental experience will be one of fear, and all its flavors. When we are connected and operating from our large, integrated and wholistic sense of self, our fundamental experience will be one of love, and all its flavors.

> One of the most important tools for your becoming and staying connected to your source of infinite safety and love, is to know the characteristics, or traits you will experience when you are connected vs. disconnected.

Hence in any moment, you can ask yourself a very basic question, "Am I coming from fear or love?"

The roots, where we are coming from, drive the fruits, the results and experiences we are having and creating in life. Actions taken from the connected, integrated-self tend to be more satisfying, productive, and efficient: often not the easy thing, but the right thing. Actions taken from the disconnected-self tend to create more work, suffering, and suboptimal results both for you and others.

Traits of the disconnected, small, separate self	Traits of the Connected, Large, Integrated Self
Flatters	Informs
Commands	Suggests
Demands	Guides
Tests	Nudges
Chooses for you	Leaves choices to you

Imprisons	Empowers
Contracted	Expanded
Promotes dependency	Promotes independence
Intrudes	Respects
Easily offended	Extends compassion
Pushes	Supports
Excludes	Includes
Status oriented and attached	Free and open
Manipulates perceptions	Courageously authentic
Focused on worst-case and avoidance	Balanced and creative
Insists on obedience	Encourages growth and development
Often claims ultimate authority	Recognizes a greater power
Offers short cuts	Offers integration
Seeks control	Seeks creative opportunity
Often in a hurry	Relaxed and trusting the process
Comes from scarcity and lack	Comes from abundance
Stingy	Generous
Seeks personal gratification	Affirms divine order along with the good of the whole
Ultimately this is all based in FEAR that disconnection perpetuates	**Ultimately this is all based in LOVE that connection perpetuates**

When we are connected to the source of life, to *our* source of life, and we know our needs for safety and love are now and forever met, our resulting thoughts, feelings, and actions create more safety and love in the world. When we are disconnected, or not connected to the source of life, we are then separate, alone, and afraid. When we are separate, alone, and afraid, our needs for safety and love are not met and we must do whatever we can or perceive we must do, to ensure they are met. The resulting thoughts, feelings, and actions typically create more separation, fear, and scarcity for you and others. There may be a perception of increased safety and love, but this is only a perception, or at best a fleeting experience that will soon end. This results in a perpetual cycle of disconnected fear-based actions and experiences.

> When we are disconnected, or not connected to the source of life, we are then separate, alone, and afraid.

The Power of Appreciation and Gratitude

As a licensed HeartMath® coach and trainer I teach people how to shift from fear to love. When I first discovered the HeartMath practices, I experienced a significant change in my awareness; from being a separate entity observing the "world out there," to being connected and integral in the world everywhere. As a trained engineer accustomed to studying systems "separate from me," it was extraordinary to experience a deep connection with all that is. A whole new world opened up for me in that moment.

One of the keys to the effectiveness of HeartMath practices, is the intentional generation of heartfelt feelings. On the continuum of heartfelt feelings, appreciation is one of the easiest to access and generate. For example, you can activate appreciation for your breath, for sunshine, for a pet, a friend, a lover, or even your favorite food. We all have things in our lives we appreciate. Bringing these things into our awareness, and activating the feeling of appreciation for them, is a powerful doorway into love as a felt experience.

> We all have things in our lives we appreciate. Bringing these things into our awareness, and activating the feeling of appreciation for them, is a powerful doorway into love as a felt experience.

It's important to activate the *feeling* of appreciation. Thinking about appreciation is not the same as feeling appreciation. The difference is significant. Feelings are felt in the body and thoughts are experienced in the head. This is the journey from our head to our heart. By activating the *feeling* of appreciation, we go beyond thinking into a felt experience of appreciation. This changes our vibration and experience in the world. It changes our TruthBubble.

Gratitude, for me, is a deeper form of appreciation. Being grateful takes our appreciation for something to a deeper level of love. We all have so much in our lives to be grateful for.

Think of our day-to-day experience in this modern world – the one we so easily take for granted - and how amazingly different it is from just a few hundred years ago. Imagine living in a one room straw hut, with a dirt floor, hunting and gathering your food, carrying your water, washing your few clothes by hand, sleeping on the ground, and doing whatever it takes to stay warm or cool. Of course, some people still live this way today.

I sometimes imagine a past life of mine where I lived in that straw hut and dreamed of what might be possible: "Someday I will live in a place with many rooms, where the temperature is controlled, cool or warm, at the flick of a switch. Where clean water is instantly available wherever I need it. It flows in both hot and cold and pours abundantly over my head. Under my feet it is soft and plush, and I sleep on something so comfortable it feels like a cloud. I have so many clothes I could wear something different every day for months, and they're cleaned with nearly no effort needed. Food is abundant and kept fresh in magical ways. Cooking is easily performed with a smokeless fire available on demand. And some cooking is done with no fire at all. I know, I know, what an impossible dream. But nonetheless, I dream it."

Trusting Things You Cannot See

A core driver of our belief in being separate and alone, and hence afraid, is our distrust or disbelief, in things we cannot see; in the metaphysical aspects of existence. This belief system has been called materialism – a belief that the only things that exist are material. Or physicalism – a belief in only physical things. This is the fundamental belief system of our western society, and due to that worldview and belief system, that TruthBubble, we use physical force to produce desired results. Take for example medicine – we use surgery to physically re-

> A core driver of our belief in being separate and alone, and hence afraid, is our distrust or disbelief, in things we cannot see; in the metaphysical aspects of existence.

move things from the body that are believed to be undesirable, or we use chemicals to change the biochemistry of the body, or we use radiation to blast and kill things. These are all physical means based in a belief system or worldview that honors or believes in only material and physical things. In this TruthBubble, nothing else exists except that which we can directly see, touch, and measure in some way, shape or form.

Over time, this is becoming a more and more ridiculous belief system and worldview. Especially since our own science of physics has proven the existence of energy fields in all matter and has shown that in fact the entire universe is far less physical or material than it at first appears. Apparently our "physical" bodies are made up of something like 99.9999% empty space. Same for the entire universe. When you look at an atom under a microscope what you mostly see is empty space. Our predominant western culture and belief system is focused on only 0.0001 % of existence and is saying "that's all there is and that's what we must work with." Hello! WTF! It's time for a serious upgrade in worldviews, belief systems and TruthBubbles.

I bring this up because the source of life itself is invisible. We cannot actually see, or even directly measure, the force of life. We see lots of its effects, like your heart beating, or a tree growing, or the earth spinning, but we do not actually see what is behind and causing these observable events. To use the healthcare system again as an example, what hospitals and doctors and nurses are doing is life *support*; they are supporting this very invisible thing called life, the mysterious thing that our cultural TruthBubbles of materialism and physicalism deny even exists! When the material aspects of the body no longer work, that is the end of life. And when *life leaves the body* all the brilliant people can do nothing about it, since we do not know what life itself is. We have not bottled it and cannot put it back in once it leaves. But while it is there, we can *support* it, and that's what the health care system is supposedly doing. Although it would deny there is any magical, miraculous aspect to this thing called life; its simply the bumping around of atoms and molecules in the body.

So, because we cannot see it, and we cannot directly measure it, even though we see its effects, we do not believe it actually exists and therefore it cannot be trusted. There are no "metaphysical forces" in which we can trust, and that's that. Here's a passage that speaks clearly and directly to this very limiting aspect of our western worldview and belief system from a Kosmos Winter 2021 Newsletter Article by Dr. Joni Carley author of *The Alchemy of Power*:

"First principles occur in the intangible realm of metaphysics, the domain of existence, being, knowing and causality. They are articulated in terms like values, morals and ethics, all of which are metaphysical distinctions. We generally overlook metaphysical factors because the paradigm in which we are all acculturated includes *fluff mythology* the fictitious belief that metaphysical factors are inconsequential fluffy stuff. There is no evidence to substantiate fluff mythology. To the contrary, the primacy of intangibles, like values and consciousness, has been demonstrated by meta-physicians, unpacked by sociologists, psychologists, philosophers and spiritual leaders throughout time, and confirmed by a plethora of international values and leadership studies across all sectors over decades. Many citations can be found in my book: The Alchemy of Power.

Fluff mythology construes metaphysics as something that has no basis in reality. But the data is clear: when metaphysical factors, like consciousness and culture, are accounted for and intentionally developed, almost all social and economic indicators go up. Fluff mythology proliferates the belief that power comes with tangibles like tanks, while it dismisses the far more formidable, yet intangible, power of our consciousness. Although rarely accounted for, consciousness determines what gets materialized and what doesn't. Consciousness is the initial condition of whatever people make happen. It is causal and determinative, yet we don't account for consciousness as the major player it is in all outcomes."

> Consciousness is the initial condition of whatever people make happen. It is causal and determinative, yet we don't account for consciousness as the major player it is in all outcomes.

In his book *The Future of God*, Deepak Chopra outlines a map for the journey of reaching God; perhaps one of the most elusive and metaphysical concepts there is! Drawing on the world's wisdom traditions and more so from the discoveries of those that have delved deep into their own consciousness, he outlines the existence of three worlds:

"**The material world.** This is the world of duality. Good and evil, light and dark contend here. Events unfold in a straight line. Each person is a tiny speck in the vastness of nature. We journey through this world driven by desire. God remains out of our reach because he is the one thing that we cannot see, touch, talk about, or conceive of. As long as we remain in duality, the ego-personality dominates. Everything revolves around 'I, me, and mine.'

The subtle world. This is the transitional world. Good and evil are not rigidly separated; light and dark merge into shades of gray. Behind the mask of materialism, we sense a presence. We move toward it using intuition and insight. Random events begin to reveal hidden patterns. We are driven through the subtle world by a craving for meaning. Nature becomes a stage setting for the soul. Everything revolves around self-awareness and its expansion.

The transcendent world. This is the source of reality itself. At the source, there is oneness, a state of unity. Nothing is divided or in conflict. The veil of materialism has fallen away completely. Good and evil, light and dark, have merged. We move through this world guided by our higher being, which is inseparable from God, who is the state of supreme being. The individual ego has expanded to become the cosmic ego. Everything revolves around pure consciousness."

This is a fascinating TruthBubble, yes? It makes sense to me, and I love its simplicity. Deepak describes some typical experiences when you touch the highest level of awareness (the transcendent world):

"You feel light, unburdened, and unbounded.

You see common humanity in every face.

You feel completely safe.

You enjoy being here for its own sake.

A calm stillness appears inside you.

Infinite possibilities seem to open up.

You feel wonder and awe looking out at nature.

You surrender, accept, and forgive.

You are certain that everything matters, things happen for a reason.

You feel that perfect freedom is the most natural way to live."

Later in the book he goes on to say:

"When you are free, silent, at peace, and completely self-aware, you inhabit the transcendent world. Labels applied to such people are *Buddha, Christ, mahatma, swami, yogi, the enlightened, the awakened.*

When you are creative, imaginative, intuitive, insightful, and inspired, you inhabit the subtle world. Labels applied to such people are *visionary, dreamer, genius, sage, seer, shaman, artist, and psychic.*

When you are involved with physical objects and sensations, you inhabit the material world. The blanket label for this is *normal.*"

It is with this intangible realm of metaphysics, the subtle and transcendent worlds, that we want to create a firm relationship. Through our path of practice, we want to move from faith, to belief, to knowing, to a day-to-day and moment to moment real world experience of these intangible realms in our very real lives. *This* is the Source of Love.

Until you are rooted in that reality, you will be on a forever treadmill of effort, struggle, and strain always trying to get your needs for safety and love met. And, at best, experiencing fleeting moments of peace before you're back on the treadmill, struggling and straining. This is the path that many follow to their awakening, to their surrender, to their discovery of this infinite source of safety and love that has been sitting right there within, waiting for them to finally come home and discover they already, and have forever, had what they need.

> When coming from our infinite source of love, our actions perpetuate love and we have an inexhaustible resource from which to give, act, and be.

It is then from this wholeness and fullness, that we can move into the world and truly be a beneficial presence on the planet. When coming from our infinite source of love, our actions perpetuate love and we have an inexhaustible resource from which to give, act, and be. Welcome home.

"If you bring forth what is within you, what you bring forth will save you. If you do not bring forth what is within you, what you do not bring forth will destroy you."

- GOSPEL OF THOMAS

References and Resources

- *Reflect*: Look again at the list of traits experienced when connected vs. disconnected. Approximately what percent of your time do you spend connected vs. disconnected? How might you increase your time and experience of being connected?
- *Read*: **Your Sacred Self – Making the Decision to Be Free, Wayne W. Dyer, 1995**

"Wayne teaches that: 1) You are sacred, and in order to know it you must transcend the old belief system you've adopted. 2) You are a divine being called to know your sacred self by mastering the keys to higher awareness. 3) Your sacred self can triumph over your ego identities and be the dominant force in your life. 4) You can radiate this awareness beyond your own boundaries and affect everyone on our planet."

- *Read*: **The Future of God – A Practical Approach to Spirituality for Our Times, Deepak Chopra, 2014**

  "God is in trouble. The rise of the militant atheist movement spearheaded by Richard Dawkins signifies, to many, that the deity is an outmoded myth in the modern world. Deepak Chopra passionately disagrees, seeing the present moment as the perfect time for making spirituality what it really should be: reliable knowledge about higher reality. Outlining a path to God that turns unbelief into the first step of awakening. Deepak shows us that a crisis of faith is like the fire we must pass through on the way to power, truth, and love."

- *Read*: **The Essentials of Theory U – Core Principles and Applications. C. Otto Scharmer, 2018**

  "Scharmer argues that our capacity to pay attention coshapes the world. What prevents us from attending to situations more effectively is that we aren't fully aware of that interior condition from which our attention and actions originate. Scharmer calls this lack of awareness our blind spot. He illuminates the blind spot in leadership today and offers hands-on methods to help change makers overcome it through the process, principles, and practices of Theory U."

- ***Read***: **The Alchemy of Power – Mastering the Invisible Factors of Leadership, Dr. Joni Carley, 2019**

  "Just like master scientists use principles of physics to transform energy into extraordinary displays of power, alchemical leaders use metaphysical principles to transform resources into results that exceed norms and expectations. Grounded squarely in data, and anchored deeply in universal wisdom, *The Alchemy of Power* reveals: what power is, what it means to have it, how to develop and manage it, and how to navigate the global call for leaders to use their power to create a better world by developing better workplaces."

- ***Watch***: **Superhuman – The Invisible Made Visible, www.Super-HumanFilm.com**

  "The *Invisible Made Visible* is based on the jaw-dropping experiences of individuals with extra-sensory powers that seem to defy the laws of physics known to man today. Producer and host Caroline Cory, who has her own extensive experience in the field of Consciousness Studies and Extra Sensory Perception, takes the viewers on an extraordinary journey to achieve tangible and measurable proof of these seemingly miraculous phenomena. Through a series of groundbreaking scientific experiments and demonstrations, viewers will find themselves connecting the dots about the true nature of their own consciousness, the relation between mind and matter and discover whether they live in a simulated matrix or if they can have control over their physical reality and create a fulfilling human experience. The film ultimately shows that once the invisible worlds are made visible, this attained higher awareness will transform humans into superhumans."

- *Listen*: **Shift It! – Accessing the Gift Within, Roger Kenneth Marsh, www.TruthBubble.com**

  This Beyond Belief Audio Program is a simple and powerful process that uses the intelligent energy and awareness of your Higher Self to transform a block, problem, or concern into an inspired opportunity…to Shift It! from one into the other. It has been designed with busy lives in mind and can be completed in less than 20 minutes.

- *Listen*: **Love Expander and Ascension Accelerator, Roger Kenneth Marsh, www.TruthBubble.com**

  This Beyond Belief Audio Program will guide you to focus on and expand the most powerful creative force in the Universe…Love. This is an experiential program that goes beyond intellectual information into the powerful world of felt experience. It has been designed with busy lives in mind and can be completed in less than 15 minutes.

Chapter 6

Seeing and Creating Your TruthBubbles

"We experience what we believe. If we don't believe that we experience what we believe, then we don't, which still means the first statement is true."

– A Course in Miracles

"Not only do I believe in being totally open-minded, I can't tolerate any other way."

– Gregg Eisenberg, Letting Go Is All We Have to Hold Onto

Your world is your mirror. To see your TruthBubbles just look at your life. What do you see, what do you experience, what are the common traits and aspects that occur on a regular basis? We are the creators of our life. However, it doesn't, at least initially, look like it.

A model for transformation, awakening, and conscious creation that I have found very valuable for this exploration is provided by

Michael Beckwith, founder of the Agape Transdenominational Spiritual Community in Culver City, California. He very simply outlines four stages of evolutionary growth that are directly related to *how* we create our TruthBubbles. It's important to know these are not linear or step-by-step in their occurrence. You can be at different stages in different areas at different times in your life. And you might bounce around a bit, a kind of one step forward, two steps back experience. Hence, hold these stages lightly and use them for inquiry to see where you may be in your life in any particular area, to see the TruthBubble you are creating:

> To see your TruthBubbles just look at your life.

Stage 1: TO ME, victim consciousness. At this stage the world is happening to us. Good luck and bad luck seem random and out of our control. Our TruthBubbles are on automatic pilot and we cannot see our role in creating them. It occurs that we are *not* creating them.

Stage 2: BY ME, manifester consciousness. At this stage we are beginning to wake up to our role in creating the results we are experiencing in our life. This stage was made popular by the documentary *The Secret* that presented this possibility of affirming things and having them occur or show up in our life. In this stage we can see our role in creating our experiences and begin to take ownership of that, we begin to be responsible for it. There is of course good news and bad news at this stage. The good news is we can create our lives and experiences, but the bad news is we are also the creators of the bad experiences and crap in our lives.

Stage 3: THROUGH ME, channel consciousness. At this stage we begin to have a deeper relationship with the divine energy flowing through us. We can see there is something bigger, deeper and wider than our "self," with a small s, that is flowing through us. We begin to let go and open up to this force, to this energy. You could say we become co-creators with it. One of the words Michael Beckwith uses for the creator is Divine Love Intelligence. I like that one. There is an intelligence at work and it has our best interests in mind. We can begin to trust this and move into greater partnership with it. At this stage we begin unlearning many of the things we may have learned about life, about ourselves, and begin surrendering and letting those go. By releasing these old TruthBubbles we begin living into new ones, channeling this higher power, intelligence, and love. We begin to see our Truth-Bubbles are co-created with the Universe itself.

Stage 4: AS ME, being consciousness. As we evolve in our awareness we can arrive at a place where there is no duality, there is no "world out there" and "me over here." There is only one thing, I am the world, I am the Universe, there is nothing that is not me, all things, everything, is me. TruthBubbles are arising of their own accord, within me, and as me, as the all and everything. There is no effort required, there is only awareness. Awareness of the isness that is all things, that is me.

We can see that the nature of our TruthBubbles, how we relate to them and our role in creating them, changes with each level. At the first stage there is no TruthBubble, there just is reality and its messing with me. Then starting at Stage 2 we begin to see our role in creating the Truth-

Bubbles we are living in. Then moving to Stages 3 and 4 "our" role as a separate entity from the world and from our TruthBubbles becomes less and less, until we literally melt into the TruthBubble. The TruthBubble and "us" become one. There is no separation, there is no actor creating the TruthBubble, it is all rising and falling in and as awareness itself.

All of these stages or levels of awareness and creation are good. All of them are fun and interesting, and valuable. It is not the goal to get to Stage 4 and stay there as long as possible. Wherever you may be, honor and enjoy it. While it might not be much fun to live in victim consciousness, we all have areas of our lives where this is true for us. We all have areas of our life experience where we believe we have no control; that the TruthBubble exists outside of us and our ability to affect it.

> **We all have areas of our life experience where we believe we have no control; that the TruthBubble exists outside of us and our ability to affect it.**

Taking an example from an earlier chapter, gravity is probably an area of your life experience where you feel you have no control over it, where you feel it is something "outside of you" that you are at effect of. You may not feel like a victim of gravity, that is a negative interpretation of your experience, however you are at Stage 1 in your consciousness with respect to your relationship with gravity; you believe you are at effect of it and not in any kind of creative relationship. And, as we saw in a previous chapter, not all people are completely "at effect" of gravity. They have moved to higher levels of consciousness and are creating a different TruthBubble than most of the people on the planet when it comes to gravity. These people may be very rare; however, they point to what's possible and pop the TruthBubble that we must be victims of some "reality out there." If we desire, we can in fact make new choices and expand our consciousness into more creative levels.

Again, we can be at various levels, in various areas of our lives. The key is to notice where we may be, notice what our TruthBubbles are, so that we can see the relationship or awareness that we have. With that awareness we can then ask if a different TruthBubble may be possible for us. Do we want a different TruthBubble than the one we are creating and experiencing? If yes, then in that moment a new possibility, a new TruthBubble is emerging. Maybe we desire to move from victim, or unconscious in our creation of a TruthBubble, to the next stage where we are going to manifest, or cause, or create a new TruthBubble, a new experience in our life with respect to this area. Here's a relatively simple, and somewhat straightforward example from my life.

Getting Closer Every Day

I hate commuting. I have done some very long ones. The longest one was sometimes 2 hours each way to work. Driving my 1990 Ford Mustang five speed into the Silicon Valley in the 1990's, stop and go, stop and go; pushing the stiff clutch in and out, was very tiring. The clothing on the back side of my body would be soaking with sweat from my leather seats when arrived! I can't stand this, I thought to myself. Living 4 hours a day in a metal coffin is no way to live, yet here I was doing it day in and day out. I knew I had to shorten my commute, and although I didn't say it this way at the time "I had seen my TruthBubble and wanted to create a new one."

Soon, it happened – I quit that job and took a job in San Francisco. Now I was driving 10 minutes, then riding BART (Bay Area Rapid Transit) for 45 minutes, then walking 10 minutes. I had cut my commute time almost in half. It still wasn't great, but it was an improvement since those minutes on BART were more my own than when driving. I lasted 6 months in that job, then quit to join a friend in a Dot Com start-up. Oh yeah.

The year was 2000 and we were going to make it big. Well, my commute shortened and I found myself with a lot more flexibility in my time and place of work – that was very nice. When I left that company, I found a job in the business park of the town I was living in. My commute was 10 minutes. Yes! Perfect! After two years in that job I quit and went back to working from home. No commute! Yes!

Then, as I went broke trying to get rich, I got a job that was a 45-minute commute. Before job hunting, I had set that as my absolute maximum commute, and that's what I got. Then, after two years in that job I quit and went back to working from home again with no commute. Yay!

And that's how it's been for the past 15 plus years, NO commute. This was an affirmation, a TruthBubble that I was creating, for about 10 years; it was a marker of something important to me and I tracked it with each emerging opportunity, more and more toward my ideal of NO commute. And now, due to the Covid19 quarantine, lots of people have joined me in the beautiful world of no commute! And beyond that, employers are increasing their accommodation and capacities to enable productive virtual teams. Awesome. TruthBubbles expanding in my world!

With this example we can see that with my 2-hour commute, which I did for about 4 years, I was at Stage 1; I was resigned and felt like a victim of this experience in my life that was out of my control, I just had to make the most of it. However, I was aware that I wanted to create a different experience. I wanted to move to Stage 2 consciousness and create a new TruthBubble with a shorter commute. I set my intention and established the clarity needed for manifesting something shorter. And guess what, when I got the job in San Francisco it occurred. With a commute of about 65 minutes, I was happy it was shorter and I could see progress, but I wanted it shorter than that.

My intention to manifest a TruthBubble at Stage 2 with a shorter commute was pretty strong. And after commuting 65 minutes for about 6 months, I then had essentially no commute since my place of work as an entrepreneur varied. Then it went to a 10-minute commute for a couple years, then up to 45 minutes for a couple years. Notice the "one step forward two steps back" phenomenon at work here. Nevertheless, I could see progress and my intention for short commutes stayed strong. Over time, I came to realize I don't like commuting at all and wanted NO commute. In fact, I don't like working in offices and would prefer working at home. I wanted to create a TruthBubble where I could have no commute and work entirely from home.

Understand that most people at this time were commuting to jobs and their places of work. It was the rare person working from home. The internet and all the possibilities we now can see was nowhere near what it is today. But my intention was clear, I was creating a new TruthBubble around this experience in my life, to the point where I am now totally working from home and have had no commute for about 10 years. Eventually I moved into a kind of Stage 3 consciousness with this area of my life as I found a beautiful co-creative partnership emerging where a bigger intelligence and guidance beyond myself was at work. I started trusting and opening to that guidance more and more.

Notice that my TruthBubble did not change overnight. TruthBubbles *can* change overnight, they can even change in an instant, however it depends on who you are and what it is you are working with.

The Laboratory of Your Life

I don't want you to believe anything I say, I want you to test it out for yourself. I encourage you to consider your life like a laboratory, where you can experiment and "see what's true for you." This is crucial. One of the main messages of this book is that we must wake up and realize that what is true for someone else does not have to be true for me and vice versa. We must learn to respect our various and unique capacities for creating our very personal and individual Truth-Bubbles. While I was able to reduce my commute time down to nothing, that might not be possible for everyone, or even desirable. Some people may actually like commuting and it may not even occur to them to shorten it. The point is, we must each discover what's true for us, and what *can* be true for us. Be your own experiment. See and explore what's uniquely true for you and if you can expand your capacities for creating new TruthBubbles in the areas that are important and relevant for you.

> One of the main messages of this book is that we must wake up and realize that what is true for someone else does not have to be true for me and vice versa. We must learn to respect our various and unique capacities for creating our very personal and individual TruthBubbles.

A Very Big TruthBubble

One big area of controversy around "what's true" is religion. Think of all the religious wars that have been, and still are, being fought over "who's religion is the true and right religion."

"The world will finally have one religion when each person has his or her own."

– Unknown

Once we realize that each person has their own TruthBubble and that we are literally experiencing and creating different worlds from each other, we'll realize how ridiculous it is to assert that there is one truth, one world, one reality "out there" that we must all agree and align on. It's not necessary and is causing a lot of suffering. We can each have and live in our own TruthBubble that is true for us, without needing anyone else to believe it, or say it's true. If something is true for us, that's all we need.

I subscribe to a magazine called *Spirituality and Health* and in that magazine is a great column by Rabbi Rami Shapiro. He answers readers' questions about religion, spirituality and other related topics. Here's one reader's question and Rabbi Rami's answer from the January / February 2021 issue:

Readers' Question: There are so many holy books: Torah, Gospels, Koran, Bhagavad Gita, Book of Mormon, Course in Miracles – can they all be true? And if not, how do I determine which among them is true.

Answer: First you have to define what is Truth. For me Truth is the four-fold teaching of Perennial Wisdom: 1) All reality is a manifesting of God called by many names: Aliveness, God, Nature, Allah, Mother, Braham, Tao, etc.; 2) Every person has the capacity to know God directly; 3) Knowing God leads to acting godly in accordance with the Golden Rule; and 4) Knowing God and acting godly is your highest calling as a human being. When a book reflects this Truth, it is true, when it doesn't, it is false. "Holy" is beside the point.

The reader's question is a good one, right? There's all these "truth claims" out there and people saying this is the one and only truth. Notice how Rabbi Rami answers this question by first defining what is true for him. He declares and owns his TruthBubble by saying "For me...." this is what's true. He doesn't claim to have "the truth," that would just be piling more crap on crap. Rather he wisely distinguishes what's true from his perspective, and then with that defined, he has a measuring stick by which these other worldviews can be compared and related to. He is offering the reader his own TruthBubble to use if they want to, to answer their question for themselves. It's now up to the reader to decide of Rabbi Rami's TruthBubble is one they want to adopt. By offering a new Truth-Bubble Rabbi Rami has offered a new possibility, even a new world, for the reader to step into.

This is a good move we can all learn to make. There is a similar approach that is recommended for Dream Circles. A Dream Circle is a group of people, usually less than ten, that meet on a regular basis to share and discuss their dreams as a way of better understanding various forces, transformations, and opportunities that may be happening in their lives. When a member of the group brings and describes a dream to others in the group, the other group members are coached to say in their replies or feedback to the dreamer "If I had that dream, this is what it would mean for me. . ." Once again, we see explicit ownership of ones TruthBubble. This allows others to now freely listen to that person describing *their* world and interpretation, and adopt what serves them and let go of what doesn't. Brilliant!

Unconscious Creations

It's important to note that sometimes it can be very difficult to see our TruthBubbles and move beyond Stage 1 consciousness to higher levels. Why? Because our TruthBubbles are being created from our unconscious minds, and because they are unconscious creations, we are not aware of our role in creating our experiences. It's important to at least consider, especially when you believe that you are not creating something, that you at least consider that you might be. You can ask, "What would have to be true about me and my beliefs, for this experience to be happening in my life. For this TruthBubble to be real for me?" This will give you a lead as to the source of your creations and where you might want to start looking, embracing, healing, releasing, and transforming.

Here's another example from my life demonstrating how TruthBubbles can be created by us without our conscious desire or awareness that we're creating them. Early on as a facilitator of groups on paths of spiritual development, I had a big discomfort leading sharing circles; circles where people are invited to share their thoughts, feelings and experiences of what is going on in their life or with the material being engaged in the program. I had a fear that someone would bring an issue that was bigger than I could handle. That they would have an emotional breakdown and I wouldn't know what to do. I feared behaving like a deer in the headlights if this were to happen to me when I had the responsibility for holding and keeping the sacred container of the sharing circle. I had seen this happen in other sharing circles where I was a participant and I was so glad that I was not the responsible facilitator needing to manage the breakdown unfolding before our eyes. Like I said, I was terrified of this.

Well, of course, because I had this fear running in me, one day in a sharing circle that I was leading, someone had a big emotional breakdown and indeed I was like a deer in the headlights. It caught me by surprise and I didn't know what to do. Fortunately, there were other caring souls in the circle and they were able to appropriately respond and facilitate the participant to a healthy place. But that didn't make me feel any better about my skills and capacity to handle whatever may come up in a circle. This happened to me a couple more times, of course.

Then I had a dream. In the dream I was on a big jet plane with 200 or so other people. The plane was going to crash and we were all going to die. As a spiritual and very caring person on the plane I felt this huge burden to save everyone on the plane. That it was my job to make sure they "got to heaven" and had a smooth transition in this fast-upcoming end of life.

The burden of this role was unbearable; there was no way I could get to all 200 people and facilitate their safe passage to the other side. Then, in the dream, there was a voice that said "It's not your job to do, they can do it for themselves, and if they can't I will do it for them, relax." Wow, what a relief, and what a major insight into the natural process of life unfolding. It's not my job to "take care of other people" and "make sure they are OK." They are always OK. There is a force of life that I can learn to trust that is flowing through all of us and will safely deliver all of us to our perfect and right destination. All I have to do is trust that, and relax.

I knew this dream was related to my fear of skillfully dealing with emotional breakdowns in a sharing circle or program. The dream showed me it's not my job, that there are higher forces at work, and that what my job actually is, is to trust, affirm, and allow THAT to unfold in the space. This was now my new TruthBubble for relating to these possible events. Once I had adopted this new belief, knowing and approach, I experienced one more emotional breakdown in a sharing circle where I was able to trust, affirm, and allow the love that heals all wounds to do its work. And it did. That was the space and energy that I now held. After that one more incident, I haven't seen another one since. And I know it's because I'm no longer "afraid" and resisting it. As we've seen, what we resist, persists. I stopped resisting, and fearing, shifted to a higher vibration, and the "problem" or experience, literally went away. I was now living in a new TruthBubble!

The Bottom Line

What truths do you want to affirm? You are the creator; you are the chooser. You don't need anyone else to believe what you believe in order for it to be true for you. You are totally free to create your own Truth-Bubbles. That doesn't mean it will be easy or fast. As we've seen there can be a lot of inertia behind the creation of our existing TruthBub-bles. However, I believe that ALL TruthBubbles can be transformed, once you can see them, once you are conscious of the TruthBubble you are creating, and then define and begin living into the new TruthBubble you prefer.

> ALL TruthBubbles can be transformed, once you can see them, once you are conscious of the TruthBubble you are creating, and then define and begin living into the new TruthBubble you prefer.

We'll now delve deeper into this process of creating TruthBubbles, explore our limits, and further distinguish the keys to their successful creation.

References and Resources

- *Reflect*: What TruthBubbles can you see that you are ready to transform? How might your life look if you no longer believed in those TruthBubbles?
- *Read*: **The Flip – Epiphanies of Mind and the Future of Knowledge, Jeffrey J. Kripal, 2019**

  "*The Flip* is Kripal's ambitious, visionary program for unifying the sciences and the humanities to expand our minds, open our hearts, and negotiate a peaceful resolution to the culture wars. Combining accounts of rationalists' spiritual awakenings and consciousness explorations by philosophers, neuroscientists, and mystics within a framework of the history of science and religion, Kripal compellingly signals a path to mending our fractured world."

- *Read*: **Life Visioning – A Transformative Process for Activating Your Unique Gifts and Highest Potential, Michael Bernard Beckwith, 2013**

  "Why have you been given this singular treasure that is your life—and how will you use it? What is the purpose for the unique blend of gifts, skills, experiences, and perspectives that you alone possess? To support you in answering these questions and living in sync with your inner calling, Michael Bernard Beckwith presents Life Visioning—an essential companion for anyone seeking to accelerate their spiritual evolution."

- *Read*: **Guinea Pig B – The 56 year experiment, R. Buckminster Fuller, 1983**

  "Buckminster Fuller whimsically labeled himself 'Guinea Pig B, B for Bucky' truly dedicating his life (from 1927 forward) to seeing what one man could do to benefit all humanity - what he termed a 50 year experiment, growing to 56 years. When he began his 'experiment' he stated that he had to expand his knowledge a great deal and unlearn a great deal more - feeling that unlearning was the most difficult discipline. It became a pursuit of rethinking everything he knew, incessantly, and saturating himself with information – 'cosmically adequate' information – considering all the possibilities, paying attention to the clues nature provides."

- *Read*: **Mind to Matter – The Astonishing Science of How Your Brain Creates Material Reality, Dawson Church, 2018**

"Every creation begins as a thought, from a symphony to a marriage to an ice cream cone to a rocket launch. When we have an intention, a complex chain of events begins in our brains. Thoughts travel as electrical impulses along neural pathways. When neurons fire together they wire together, creating electromagnetic fields. The fields are invisible energy, yet they influence the molecules of matter around us the way a magnet organizes iron filings. In *Mind to Matter*, award-winning researcher Dawson Church explains the science showing how our minds create matter. We can now trace the science behind each link in the chain from thought to thing, showing the surprising ways in which our intentions create the material world."

- *Listen*: **Deep Relaxation and Power Visioning Process, Roger Kenneth Marsh, www.TruthBubble.com**

  This Beyond Belief Audio Program will leave you feeling refreshed and relaxed, powerfully present to your deepest life desires and ready for whatever awaits you. The program provides a structure inside of which you will deeply visualize and energize your desired "parallel realities," calling them into existence and into your experience. By doing this you are employing one of your most powerful and fundamental "God given gifts," to create and manifest your life's desires.

Chapter 7

Envelopes of Influence

"During those times as we've seen in our stories, what we intend happens and what happens is what we intend. There is no waiting, since everything is already taking place. There is no unfulfilled desire, since desire itself dissolves on the ever-present instant of fulfillment. There are no chance events, since we are the architects of creation and all things are connected through us. Others around us, other universes, report that they too are affected. Miracles seem to happen, eventually seeming less like miracles than "just the way things are." The ego is not destroyed or distressed, as in schizophrenia, but transcended. Each of us, in this ultimate interplay, is like a god, omnipotent and omniscient. Does this mean we can fly or move mountains? It's impossible to say. But whatever happens is just what is intended. In the playground of reality, where the relationship between identity and holonomy is directly experienced, each of us is in the business of creating all of existence, effortlessly, on the wink of an instant."

- George Leonard, The Silent Pulse

Exploring the Limits

Can we fly or move mountains? Good question! In the quote above, George asks this question from a place of authentic and open curiosity. You can feel his supportive nature in the words he has written. As a pioneer in human potential, George was asking an honest question. And, while he says each of us *is* in the business of creating all of existence, when it comes to flying and moving mountains, his answer "It's impossible to say," leaves it open for our discovery.

On the other side of this open and supportive inquiry we have the skeptic. The skeptic asks a question like "Can we fly or move mountains?" from a place of doubt. The skeptic already knows it's not possible and is out to prove it. Skeptics will often go to extremes in their attempt to maintain the perceived safety of their own TruthBubble.

Since we all have our own skeptic within us, let's look more closely at the objections of our skeptic. When a skeptic engages this material, the question might be "If we create our own reality, then why aren't you a millionaire that can levitate and walk-through walls?" The logic here is basically that if I have not created or cannot do those things, then we cannot or do not create our own realities. Like most black and white, either/or thinking, it's flawed. The fact that I am not a millionaire, cannot levitate or walk-through walls, does not prove that we do not create our reality and experience in life.

Why not? Well, first, it assumes I want those things. While it may be nice to have and do those things, none of them are absolutely essential for me to fully live my soul's purpose and experi-

> Your soul does not want to waste time doing things it did not come here to do.

ence the life I am here to live. I don't desire them in ways that would motivate me to achieve and have them. In my experience the capacity to create your reality is related to your soul's purpose and your reason for being alive. Your soul does not want to waste time doing things it did not come here to do.

Second, this skeptic's test also does not reflect and take into account the more than likely long-term path of practice needed to manifest such extreme and relatively unusual outcomes in our time. There is an unspoken, unrealistic, and unconscious assumption in the question which goes something like "If we create our realities, that means we can instantaneously create anything we want, otherwise it's just regular old normal creation that happens over time. Nothing new and no magic there."

Let's be clear, I am not saying you can create anything you want and that it will happen instantaneously. While I do believe *anything is* possible and I would never put any limit on anyone's possible TruthBubbles, the likelihood of creating any TruthBubble is *relative* and it *depends*. It's *relative* to 1) your current TruthBubbles and the evolutionary leap you are navigating and 2) to the time or epoch you live in on the planet and what is generally possible for most of humanity during that time (more on this later). In addition, it *depends* on you and your very unique and personal capacities for creating your TruthBubbles. As we've seen, what's possible for you may not be possible for others, and what's possible for others may not be possible for you...it depends.

> It's an immature perspective to expect everything instantaneously. The more mature perspective recognizes, yes, anything is possible, and there is a path you must walk for its unfolding and realization.

These are not qualifiers trying to hedge on the ultimate message of this book. These are distinctions that allow us to better and more wisely navigate into and create our own, relevant TruthBubbles. It's an immature perspective to expect everything instantaneously. The more mature perspective recognizes, yes, anything is possible, *and* there is a path you must walk for its unfolding and realization.

This is very different than the materialist's perspective that what is possible is limited by physical reality and occurs within a very narrow band of mostly already discovered and well-worn pathways. Skeptical naysayers play within very small, seemingly safe and predictable worlds and habitually shut down others who dare to venture beyond those worlds. They do this because it threatens their worldview and, since worldview is often tied up and equated with who one is, it threatens their existence; their access to the safety and love they need. It's totally understandable why they would try to discredit a worldview that apparently threatens their own.

Nonetheless, it's important to see that the materialist's perspective is just one extreme TruthBubble where what's possible is only what has been done before. The other end of this spectrum is insisting that if we do create our realities then that means "anything is possible instantaneously." This is just the other extreme TruthBubble which is just as unbalanced and unreasonable as the first. What we are looking for is a more balanced approach and perspective that honors both our own, and others, current and future capacities to create new realities. We could call this "the middle path" where we avoid the pitfalls of extremes while at the same time respecting and being informed by the limitations they suggest, e.g., we don't create our reality vs. we can instantaneously create any reality we want. The truth is somewhere in the middle.

The Benefits of Space and Time

I've listened a fair amount to Bashar who is an off-planet channeled entity by a living man named Darryl Anka. This may sound crazy to you, however keep in mind the message of this book: we are creating our own TruthBubbles, everything that shows up in them is a mirror of us and is there for a reason. Bashar may or may not be an actual off-planet living entity, but it doesn't matter to me. Just like anything that comes into my world, my TruthBubble, I sort and filter and potentially integrate it based on my personal felt sense of its value *for me*. And for me, what's valuable are things that help me live my most authentic and fulfilling life more fully and freely, and become the most beneficial presence on the planet I can become. Pretty much everything Bashar says meets these criteria for me, hence I pay attention to what he is saying and use it in my own life. The fact he just might be an evolved, conscious entity from our very distant future makes it more fascinating and interesting, but isn't the criteria I am using to validate the value of his messages.

Like our skeptic in this chapter many of Bashar's students also desire to instantaneously create anything they want and get frustrated when they can't. So, they ask Bashar, who says we are in fact creating our own realities every instant, why this is so. One of his answers really stuck with me. It is that we have incarnated into this particular dimension of space and time because we *want* to experience a more slowly unfolding reality. We *want* to enjoy the journey and the discovery over time as the creator of our experience and outcomes. We like and want to experience the creative journey over time and through space.

In other realities and dimensions Bashar says things manifest much more quickly, but here we have intentionally chosen a slower process of

tion. And, apparently this is one of the more difficult realities to
n since there are longer delays between our thoughts and feelings
and their reflection back to us in our world. It's harder to see the connection between what we think and feel and the results and experiences
in our life. Especially when you take into account the creative influence
of our unconscious minds, that by definition we are unconscious and
unaware of.

Bashar provided the example of visiting a dear friend or family member living a couple thousand miles away. Imagine that you instantaneously
teleport yourself from your home to theirs and are now with them and
visiting. Might be pretty great right? Boom, there you are. Now, imagine
you invest a day to travel and maybe a thousand dollars in expenses including a 3- or 4-hour flight to visit them. When you arrive imagine how
the visit will be different. Next, consider that you drive for 3 or 4 days
to visit your friend. You invest in all the gas, wear and tear on your car,
hotels and meals along the way. Imagine how your arrival and time with
them will be different by traveling to see them in this manner. Finally,
and Bashar did not provide this example, but I find it interesting to consider, imagine you *walk* the 2,000 miles to visit your friend. You are so
committed to seeing them you are willing to walk the entire 2,000 miles
just to see them. If you walked 30 miles every day you could get there in
about two months. Imagine what your arrival and time with them would
be like after a two-month journey fully committed and invested in seeing
and being with them.

Reflecting on this example you can see that while instantaneous manifestation might be great, there is also great value in the process and journey
of creation through the unique time and space continuum we exist in.
With this kind of awareness, we can come to appreciate and enjoy the pro-

cess, grateful for each step and each moment, and allow our desired TruthBubbles
to emerge and unfold in their own perfect
and right timing, with no rush. In this context the journey is just as important as the
arrival, and the arrival is made even more
sweet by savoring the journey.

> The journey is just as important as the arrival, and the arrival is made even more sweet by savoring the journey.

Now, back to our question posed by George Leonard, can we fly or move mountains? Or can we become a millionaire, levitate and walk-through walls? What is "the truth" regarding our possibilities? Are there any limits and if so where are they and why are they?

Your Personal Envelope of Influence

"God grant me the serenity to accept the things I cannot change, the courage to change the things I can, and the wisdom to know the difference."

- THE SERENITY PRAYER

We each have our own, what I've come to call, "envelope of influence." Your envelope of influence is the extent of your power, or your capacity, to shape and create your reality. We must each discover for ourselves the extent of our capacities. And to do this we must *experiment* to find out; to feel into and begin knowing where the edges of our envelope of influence are.

This is a dynamic element, it is changing. What was at one point in your life the edge of your envelope, you may have gone beyond and now have far more capacity to shape and influence your reality. You won't know this until you try, until you test and see how your inner world impacts your outer world and you look into that mirror. We must test to see the shape and extent of our TruthBubble: Where are its edges? What is clearly inside your TruthBubble, where you have

> What was at one point in your life the edge of your envelope, you may have gone beyond and now have far more capacity to shape and influence your reality.

capacity to shape and create, and what's outside, where you have less or apparently no influence to shape and create it?

You've probably heard various stories told in personal development arenas that are intended to inspire us; to help us courageously move beyond what we have thought is possible. Or, in the language of this book, to test a TruthBubble that *was* true for us and see if it is *still* true. I'd like to remind us of a couple of these stories. I do not know for sure if these things are true, I have not tested them myself, however the point they make is still relevant.

Apparently when an elephant is small and young, the elephant trainers will put a rope or chain around one of their legs and tie it to a stake in the ground they cannot pull out. When the small, young elephant tries to pull away from the stake, they cannot do it and they must therefore stay within the range their rope or chain allows. Over time, after various attempts at trying to move away from the stake, they eventually learn their efforts are futile and they stop trying. This mindset is then carried forward their entire life. When they grow up into huge and powerful animals, they still do not try to remove the stake and move beyond the limits of their rope or chain, even though now they are completely capable of just walking away from the stake and easily pulling it out. Just a little tug on their leg has them stay in their small circle. They are stuck in a mental model from their childhood, their TruthBubble was formed and they are still living inside it. Even though now, their TruthBubble, or envelope of influence, is *far* bigger than it used to be. Unless they really tested it and went beyond the limits they previously experienced, they will never know.

The second example is fleas in a jar. If you put fleas in a jar they will try to jump out. But if you put a lid on the jar, they will bump up against the lid for some period of time trying to escape. Eventually because they're smart fleas, tired of banging their heads on the lid, they stop trying. At this point, apparently, you can take the lid off and the fleas will stay in the jar; they will not try to jump out and escape. However, reality has changed and what is possible for them has changed, but they are stuck in the TruthBubble originally experienced and created.

These two examples are interesting because in the first one it is the elephant that has changed. The external reality (the chain and the stake) has not changed, but the elephant's capacity, their strength and size, has significantly changed. This growth in personal capacity of the elephant has gone unnoticed on their part, at least when it comes to escaping the stake.

In our second example, it's the external world that has changed. The capacity of the flea to jump is the same, however the external world (the lid being removed) has changed and they don't know it, or don't trust there is anything different.

In both examples, the creatures have created a TruthBubble they are now unwilling, or don't know, they can change. Our lives are just like this. Sometimes we personally change and have new capacities we're unaware of, and sometimes the external world has changed and what was once not possible for us is now possible. Either way we will not know we can expand our TruthBubble, that we can live into whole new possibilities and realities, unless we are willing to test our reality, explore our envelope of influence, and risk creating a *new* TruthBubble.

It takes courage to test the extent of our TruthBubbles. For those poor little fleas, do they really want to bang their head on the lid again? No! But how will they know if the lid is there or not unless they try. I don't know why they cannot *see* that the lid is gone. Seems it would be a much easier and safer way to explore their

> It takes courage to test the extent of our TruthBubbles.

limits – just look up! Nonetheless, it seems the only way they can know is if they jump again, one more time. We have lots of metaphorical lids in our lives that we cannot see, that require us to take action to test and see if they are still there, or if there is new freedom and capacity available to explore.

Levels of Consciousness Impact Your Envelope

As we saw in the previous chapter, *Seeing and Creating TruthBubbles*, an important part of our capacity to create our reality is our conscious awareness of reality itself and how we see our creative role in that reality – victim, manifester, channel, or being. In general, our envelope of influence gets bigger with each expanded level of consciousness. And, interestingly, at the same time our desire to *change* reality goes down since we are more at peace with exactly how things are. Often, we want to change things because we're not happy, we need something to be different *so that* then we can be happy.

At the victim level of consciousness, we want the pain and suffering of being a victim to stop – that's normal, and that's motivating! At the manifester level, we typically want to get and achieve things so that we can be happy, safe and loved. At the channel level of consciousness, we begin letting go of our attachments to *how things need to be in order for me to be happy* and we start knowing and trusting the divine, guiding intelligence of the universe. We start seeing that the universe is happening for us. We don't have to "do anything to it," just surrender and let go and allow, more and more. Our envelope of influence has greatly expanded as we allow the universe itself to guide us to what's next. This is more along the lines of the old saying "thy will be done, not mine," since we are realizing thy will and my will, are more and more the same.

As we arrive in oneness there is no thy or my, it's all one and the same. You might even say the envelope or TruthBubble disappears at this level since there is no inside or outside to be experienced. It's all the same, it's all *in*, there is no outside or other to be seen. There is no "edge" of the bubble or envelope, YOU ARE THE UNIVERSE, the whole thing, inside and out. Cause and effect are irrelevant, there is simply rising and falling, a constant dance of energy coming and going, in, through and as you.

The following image represents another model or framework to help distinguish where your envelope of influence may reside. It's from a book called *The Intelligent Heart*, by Bruce and David McArthur. The model shows three dimensions of energetic manifestation; the 3rd, the 4th, and the 5th. As you rise in dimensions, your power and influence to shape and change the physical world increases. Developing love consciousness and love intelligence – engaging "The Law of Love" – is the access to higher dimensions.

The 3rd dimension represents the physical world and a worldview that is focused on one's self and the material world. In the Lower 4th dimension, the awareness that "we are interdependent" rises, resulting in a sense of social responsibility, but there is still relatively low impact of one's consciousness on reality and therefore there is relatively slow change. As we move up to the Middle 4th dimension, the realization "I create my reality" dawns, and we begin a path of inner world change and transformation. There is effect on the 3rd dimension but it is still relatively weak. As we move to the Higher 4th dimension, which is accessed through the heart, our efficiency and power increase and we start to have greater impact and ability to change the 3rd dimension. Finally, in the 5th dimension, where one's Divine purpose is being followed and realized, we have a very strong impact on the 3rd dimension.

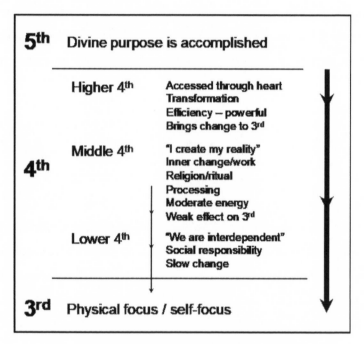

Source: "The Intelligent Heart," David McArthur &
Bruce McArthur, A.R.E Press, © 1997

We can look at the impact of our consciousness on our capacity to create TruthBubbles in one more way by returning to the "Three Worlds" model provided by Deepak Chopra in his book *The Future of God*, that we outlined in Chapter 5. As Deepak says "A creator is constantly making possibilities come true. All that it takes is to be comfortable in all three worlds of the creative process:

Transcendent world: You are comfortable here when you can experience all possibilities. Your awareness is open. You are connected to the source. Your consciousness is merged with the mind of God.

Subtle world: You are comfortable here when you can hold on to your vision. You trust yourself to follow where the mind goes. You aren't bound up in resistance, objections, skepticism, and rigid beliefs. Inspiration occurs as a normal part of your existence.

Material world: You are comfortable with your personal reality. You take responsibility for it. You read the world as a reflection of who you are and what is happening "in here." As the reflection shifts and changes, you track the changes occurring inside yourself."

Remember, that while having models, frameworks and maps for things like levels of consciousness and their impact on our creative capacities can be very helpful, we must remember these are also TruthBubbles. The map is not the terrain itself. We must travel these paths ourselves to determine the helpfulness of the maps and bring them alive in our own experience.

Expanding Consciousness on a Cosmic Scale - Consider The Yugas

The yugas are a tradition in India that goes back thousands of years. In the Introduction to their book *The Yugas – Keys to Understanding Our Hidden Past, Emerging Energy Age, and Enlightened Future*, authors Joseph Selbie and David Steinmetz write, "In the Holy Science, Sri Yukteswar describes a recurring cycle of human development, called the cycle of the yugas, or ages. The complete cycle is made up of an ascending half, or arc, and a descending half, or arc, each lasting 12,000 years. In the ascending arc of 12,000 years, mankind evolves through four distinct ages, or yugas, reaches the peak of development, and then devolves through the four ages, in reverse order, in another 12,000 years of the descending arc. Thus, in the course of 24,000 years, mankind as a whole rises in knowledge and awareness, and again falls, in a cycle that occurs again and again."

Further, they say "Sri Yukteswar explains that the cycle of the yugas is caused by influences from outside our solar system that affect the *consciousness* of all mankind. As mankind's consciousness changes as a result of this influence, so also does mankind's perception, awareness, and intellect. In the higher ages that Sri Yukteswar describes, mankind not only knows more but is able to perceive more than we do today; mankind as a whole not only has more advanced capabilities but becomes motivated profoundly differently as the ages unfold. In the higher ages described by Sri Yukteswar, perceptions and abilities considered highly unusual today, will be as normal to everyone alive at that time, as cars, planes, and telephones are to us today."

You might at first consider the concept of the yugas as a limiting one since mankind's consciousness is determined by forces outside our control. And, while it's true that the "lower stages" of the cycle can be limiting to our consciousness and capabilities, what the overall model shows us is what's possible for us as human beings. And, that as a species, we've been there before! Consider the general consciousness and awareness of the universe at each level:

- Kali Yuga: material awareness only; everything is physical and that's it

- Dwapara Yuga: energy underlies the material; everything is energy
- Treta Yuga: thought underlies energy which underlies the material; everything is thought
- Satya Yuga: Spirit/God underlies thought which underlies energy which underlies the material; everything is Spirit/God

We are in the early phases of the Dwapara Yuga, entering into the energy age, and we are on the ascending part of the overall cycle. We can see evidence of this in things like Albert Einstein's introduction of $E=mc^2$ in 1905 fundamentally changing our consciousness, our awareness, by demonstrating that all matter is essentially condensed energy. Notice that this discovery was

The overall consciousness of the average person still does not include the awareness that *everything* is energy.

made more than 100 years ago and that the overall consciousness of the average person still does not include the awareness that *everything* is energy. We are still at the very beginning stages of understanding what this actually means and how it changes *everything* we do; we are still very much stuck in materialism.

However, just because most of the world is living in a TruthBubble that says everything is matter, still stuck in the consciousness of the Kali Yuga, that does not mean *we* must live there too! Through practices such as those offered in this book, we can develop the consciousness and awareness of Dwapara, Treta, and even Satya Yugas.

Our science has already demonstrated that everything is energy and it's beginning to show us, with experiments like the double slit experiment, that our thoughts and observations have a role to play. Eventually, as we come to understand that we live in an intelligent, ever evolving Universe, we'll come to understand that intelligence itself is what underlies all things. But we don't have to wait for "someday," or for 12,000 years to pass! While developing this kind of awareness, consciousness, and capabilities will be much easier in those more advanced ages, we can still do it today.

> Our science has already demonstrated that everything is energy and it's beginning to show us, with experiments like the double slit experiment, that our thoughts and observations have a role to play.

Another reason why the cycle of the yugas makes sense to me is that it mirrors on a very large scale the cycles we see on smaller scales. Related to the old saying "That which is above is like that which is below, and that which is below is like that which is above," it's obvious that life cycles. We can see small cycles like our breath going in and out, and our heart beat with its contraction and expansion. We can see slightly larger cycles with day turning into night and vice versa, and the movement of the seasons from a contracted winter phase to an expanded summer phase. It makes sense to me that these cycles would expand up to larger and larger levels like those of the yugas.

The book that Joseph and David wrote is excellent! They put together an incredibly compelling body of evidence supporting the existence of this cycle of yugas. You don't have to be a genius to know there are existing accomplishments of previous generations on this planet that we do not fully understand. We need look no further than the megalithic creations of 1,000s of years ago. Our ancestors moved unreasonably large and extraordinary amounts of solid stone for hundreds of miles, sometimes up mountains, then stacked them on top of each other like little bricks. If you live in a linear TruthBubble (vs. a cyclical one) that says we are the most advanced people that have ever lived and that all previous generations were "primitive" with respect to us, then you must explain what you see through the only lens you have. In most cases, with these extraordinary accomplishments, that explanation is "we really don't know how they did it."

Real World Practices

Getting Clarity - Wish, Want, Walk

Let's look at some real-world practices for feeling into your envelope of influence in day-to-day life. One area rich with opportunity is any time you're going to buy something, especially if the price to be paid is negotiable or is unknown to you. Before entering into negotiation where the price will be determined, you can do a simple internal reflection process to determine what TruthBubble you want to create and experience when it comes to the price you will pay. I learned this from T. Harv Eker, author of the book *Secrets of the Millionaire Mind*, in one of his amazing training programs when he ran Peak Potentials Training. He called it the "Wish, Want, Walk" approach to negotiation.

The first thing you ask yourself is "What do I wish this product or service will cost me?" This is your best-case scenario. What is the price you will be *thrilled* to get the product or service for? You might say "well, isn't that always going to be free? Or THEY pay me to take it?" Maybe, but usually not. You have to feel into your truth here. If there is value to you in the product or service, that value should be respected and honored and the appropriate energy should be reflected back to the person providing the product or service. You also want to take into account who the seller is, your capacity to pay, and the relationship between you and the seller. So, your wish price is a great price for you, *and* it respects the other person or entity offering the product or service. It's still a win/win for both of you, it's just that it makes you very happy given you feel the value you're receiving is more than the price you're paying.

Your second question is "What do I *want* to pay for this product or service?" What do you feel is reasonable given all you know about what the product or service is probably worth on the open market, the need of the seller to receive remuneration, and your ability to pay? What would you be willing to pay and still be happy with the exchange? This is your realistic price, the one most likely to be offered by the seller, the one most expected, since it is not too much, it is not too little, and is likely appropriate given market conditions and willingness of other buyers to pay that price.

Finally, ask yourself "At what price do I walk away and not purchase the product or service?" Where is your "no way, that's too much" limit? With these three amounts, or TruthBubbles of experience, clear in your mind you can now approach the seller and ask "How much is this product or service?" It's always good to see where they are starting, and if they hit your wish or want price, boom, you've got a deal and you are happy. If they come in higher than your want price you can of course ask if they would take your want price. You can see if there is room for negotiation by letting them know what you are willing to pay. Of course, you can start with your wish price and go up from there. If they say yes, then again you are happy, they are happy, and you've got a deal.

I've played this game many, many times in my life, and it's surprising how often my wish price is delivered. The want price also happens a fair amount, and the walk price less so, but still happens. I feel that by establishing this clarity in my mind, that by "declaring to the universe" here's where my TruthBubble stands, the universe then responds in kind. I find that if I do not do this, my experience of miracles occurs less often, e.g., prices are either what I would expect or way too much.

Here's one example of this TruthBubble practice that really stood out for me. I was on a business trip to Houston Texas. Coming from California, where the weather was perfect, I forgot my umbrella. It often rains in Houston, and when it rains it pours. I needed to walk about four blocks to the office where I was working and I knew I was going to need an umbrella.

I went into the hotel gift shop looking around hoping to find an umbrella and found that yes, they had one, and ONLY one. I was super happy to find this umbrella there. It was exactly what I wanted and was looking for. One of the small, compact black umbrellas that pop up and then fold down neatly into an easy to carry unit. This was the only one there and it had no price on it, nowhere could I find a price.

I thought to myself, what are my wish, want and walk prices? As you might imagine, given that it was pouring rain outside and I did not want to show up in the office soaking wet, the value of this umbrella to me was pretty high. But still, I did not want to get ripped off (which as you know can be the case with these "last minute needs" convenience shops). I thought to myself, I'm willing to pay up to $25.00 for this umbrella, plus tax, but anything higher than that and I will find another option. That was my walk price limit. I *want* it to cost less than $15.00. That was my want price. And it would be great if it was like five bucks or something less. That was my wish price.

With my wish, want and walk prices clearly defined in my consciousness, I took the umbrella to the register and said to the woman there, "How much is this umbrella? There is no price on it." She looked it over and yes, confirmed there was no price. She then called out to a coworker asking "Do you know what the price is for this umbrella?" No, was the response. After a few more seconds of pondering the situation, the clerk rang it up and said "How about two dollars?" I was blown away. I said "Are you sure? I mean, that works for me, I'm happy to pay $2 for this umbrella if that works for you?" And she said yes. So I gave her $2 dollars and went happily on my way having gotten even better than my wish price of $5.00.

For me this was a clear demonstration of my envelope of influence and power of my TruthBubble. The probability of that umbrella actually being $2.00 is near nil. And the probability that the staff there would give it to me for $2.00 is also near nil. But it happened! This is not something that you would expect, it's beyond predictable, and hence why it was so meaningful for me. The wish, want, walk process is just one simple way and example that you can use to test and shape your envelope of influence and TruthBubbles.

Non-Attachment

I think part of the reason the wish, want, walk process works is because you're not demanding and attached to a specific or particular outcome; you're flexible, the universe has options for its response. You know you *might* experience a "walk" price, and you're ok with that, you've got a plan B and can meet your needs in other ways. It's important that you're not attached; you're free, you're OK, you're whole and complete, not needy or weak. You're coming from a place of clarity and power. It has been said that as soon as you don't need something you can then ac-

> It has been said that as soon as you don't need something you can then actually have it.

tually have it. The wish, want, walk process can be applied to pretty much any area of life where you can define the outcomes in that manner so you're clear and intentional prior to engaging and negotiating an outcome.

As mentioned in a previous chapter, Landmark Education is a company that offers The Landmark Forum. It's an evolution of Werner Erhard's EST program (Erhard Seminars and Training). One of their distinctions for creating desired realities is to realize that "Expectations lead to upset." Their coaching is to take a stand for a possibility. You're committed to the possibility, but not attached, and since you are not attached, if things unfold in different ways than the way you saw it with your possibility, you're not upset; you can pivot and follow new directions unfolding. These new directions may ultimately lead to your desired outcome or possibility in new ways, or to a different possibility or outcome that is even better. If you're attached, you can't see new opportunities unfolding since you're only looking for one thing, in one way.

Discovery Through Action

We can begin to see our envelopes of influence in all areas of our life by experimenting with them. Looking back at my example given when I quit my job, my envelope of influence, my TruthBubble, was way bigger than I realized. The company was happy to have me as a part-time consultant if the choice I was offering

> We can begin to see our envelopes of influence in all areas of our life by experimenting with them.

them was part-time or nothing. It's important to notice I was ok and willing to engage the "nothing" option. Also, I wasn't demanding the part-time option; in fact I didn't even know it was possible. But with the nudge from my friend, and the request from my boss, it unfolded in a beautiful way and my TruthBubble has been bigger because of that ever since.

Where is your envelope of influence, your TruthBubble with your:

- Health?
- Finances?
- Employment, job, or career?
- Relationships?
- Freedom (to be who you are and do what you love)?
- Family?
- Children (If you have them)?
- Any area of your life that is important to you?

You can begin paying attention to how you are creating your experience by looking at and paying attention to what you are experiencing. The universe is a perfect mirror for your TruthBubble, for how you are seeing and holding your world to be true. As it has been said, if you look in the mirror and see an unhappy, frowning face, you don't go over to the mirror and try to put the happy face on over there. The only way to change that reflection is by you changing yourself, right where you are, and smiling.

> The universe is a perfect mirror for your TruthBubble, for how you are seeing and holding your world to be true.

All too often people get busy trying to "change the world out there," trying to change the reflection in the mirror, and it doesn't work. Or if it does, it's temporary. Lasting change is sourced from within. Changing a TruthBubble starts with changing yourself. Depending on the changes in the mirror you are seeking, this may take a long time or a short time. But either way, by focusing on yourself, and diligently, patiently, practicing and affirming the changes you wish to see in the mirror, they will eventually show up. And when they do, you know you've changed your TruthBubble, you've expanded your envelope of influence.

Wanting the Highest and Best for Everyone

Another tip for expanding your TruthBubble and envelope of influence, is wanting the highest and best for all involved. This is rooting in an energy of love and appreciation for others. This is a very powerful perspective to take as you develop capacity to expand your TruthBubbles. When you affirm the highest and best for all involved, you are engaging the most powerful evolutionary force there is, that of evolutionary love. You do not want to expand your TruthBubble at the expense of others; you want the expansion of your TruthBubble to contribute to and expand the TruthBubbles of others. This is a very good energy to affirm as you go about your work expanding your envelope of influence; that you will be a beneficial presence on the planet and the expansion of your TruthBubble expands all others.

Going with the Flow

Here's another example of an experience I had in day-to-day life allowing the universe to support me and trusting the unfolding of experiences. This is an example of "going with the flow" or "flowing with the go" – another powerful practice for expanding your envelope of influence.

I had placed an order for pick up at my favorite local pizza place. I waited the amount of time they said it would take and showed up to pick up my pizza. When I got there, the place was very busy. They said it was not quite ready and asked me to wait a few more minutes. I took a seat at the bar near the register and, while not exactly happy it wasn't ready, I was fine to wait a few more minutes. After about 10 minutes they brought the box to me and presented it proudly, "Here you are sir." I was relieved and ready to go but thought to just take a peek into the box to confirm it was what I ordered. What I wanted to see was a beautiful pepperoni and black olive pizza, but what I saw was plain cheese. Uh oh.

I immediately flagged down the waiter and said this was not my order. He confirmed that indeed I had ordered pepperoni and black olive and that this was plain cheese. He apologized and said he would put that order in right way and asked if I would like something to drink while I waited. Well, I figured a pizza, especially when the place is super busy, will take about 20 minutes, so I ordered one of my favorite draft beers and relaxed into my seat. Was I happy to wait another 20 minutes? No! But these things happen. I was comfortable in my seat, had one of my favorite draft beers, and no one was urgently waiting for me to bring home the pizza.

As I finished the beer, at about the 20-minute mark up came my pizza. When I peaked in I saw the deliciously sizzling hot pepperoni and black olives looking so perfect right out of the oven. As I went for my wallet to pay for the beer, the bartender said it's on the house, and so is the additional cheese pizza. This is a gourmet, family owned, one of a kind pizza place. Their cheese pizza with no toppings starts at $20. So, with my patience, peacefulness, and trust of the Universe that all things are happening for me, not against me, I was rewarded with almost $30 in free food and drink. And, my originally ordered pizza could not have been hotter and fresher.

That experience could have gone many different ways, had I not been willing to go with the flow; had I actively resisted what was occurring. There are people who would have felt personally slighted at the mistake and would've potentially demanded everything be free. There could've been a scene and tension created in the restaurant as the second pizza was being made. Or someone might have gotten all the way home and THEN realized it wasn't what they ordered. At that point, either you eat the pizza you got, or you go through a lot more hassle to get the one you originally ordered. This could be a trauma that puts that pizza place on one's personal black list for a long time! However, through patience, understanding, affirming and trusting that everything happens for a reason and that reason is there to serve you, we can indeed live into beautiful TruthBubbles and expand our envelopes of influence in the most simple and basic places in our everyday lives.

What About the Big Things?

OK Roger, you might say, this is all fine and good when it comes to umbrellas and pizzas, but what about the big things in life, the big TruthBubbles we're living in? How do we test and know the limits of those? Well, good question. I might at first turn that around and ask you for your thoughts on that one, how do you know the limits of your TruthBubbles, *all* of them? Maybe give that a moment or two of reflection. Take out a piece of paper and answer this question: How do I know the limits of my TruthBubbles in all areas of my life, especially the areas I consider the BIG ones? Write down your thoughts and then compare your notes with what I offer in what follows.

OK, got your thoughts? Great. Let's explore this a bit more. One of the things I've said to people as I've gotten into these types of conversations is "Before you jump off a 10-story building expecting to fly, I'd try jumping off a few things much, much lower." As I've stated before, the force of gravity and its very predictable impact on us as humans is a TruthBubble that is very rooted in

> Before you jump off a 10-story building expecting to fly, I'd try jumping off a few things much, much lower.

humanity and our experience. To create a whole new TruthBubble where one is free of the force of gravity would be considered an absolute miracle – far beyond one's capacity to get near free umbrellas, pizza and beer. So, let's look at the underlying mechanics in expanding one's TruthBubble and envelope of influence in the big or more widely "already determined" areas of life experience.

Believe Something Else May Be Possible

The first and very important step is to allow yourself to believe something else may be possible. For example, "I might be able to fly if I jump off a 10-story building." No matter how solid or real or "true" something supposedly is, e.g., if I jump off a 10-story building I will fall to the ground and die - if you can allow yourself to believe that another TruthBubble may be possible, this is your first step toward the successful creation of that new possibility and TruthBubble. As long as you believe in the current or existing reality for you, there is no other possibility; you are like the fleas in the jar or the elephant tied to the stake.

> If you can allow yourself to believe that another TruthBubble may be possible, this is your first step toward the successful creation of that new possibility and TruthBubble.

Get Clear on the What, the Why, and the Impact

Having embraced that something new might be possible, you can then embark on your adventure to explore. Starting with "What TruthBubble would you like to affirm, create, and experience? And why?" Getting clarity on what TruthBubble you would like to create and *why* you want to create it is very important. If the TruthBubble I wanted to create is "I can jump off a 10-story building and fly," it's important to ask why would I want to do that? If my reason for wanting to jump off a 10-story building and fly is based in an ego need to get love, feel powerful, or impress other people, it's a very weak reason for creating that TruthBubble. But if it is somehow *very* relevant to my existence, to my soul's purpose, to my life's purpose, then it may be a TruthBubble I may actually have access to and I may want to begin creating.

Michael Murphy, co-founder of Esalen Institute and author of many books including *The Future of the Body – Explorations into the Further Evolution of Human Nature*, said once in a seminar I was attending, "Watch out for metaphysical hernias. We need wisdom to inform our practice and the goals we establish." He went on to recommend, "We must look for our dharma lines, our perennial interests. It doesn't matter how far we get, what matters is that we are going in the right direction. It will be highly individual; not everyone doing the same thing."

It's hard to imagine what the dharma lines, or the soul's purpose of a person might be that would have as an imperative the ability to jump off a 10-story building and fly. What comes to mind for me is that person may be the prototype or first person demonstrating a whole new capacity for humanity to free themselves from gravity and move about the world with no extra apparatus needed. If that was your soul's purpose, and your life was about creating and demonstrating this whole new TruthBubble, you will feel it and you will start making progress toward its realization.

It was once believed that a person could not run faster than a four-minute mile, that it was beyond human capacity. No one had ever done it and it was deemed impossible. However, in 1954 Roger Bannister did it. An example of the impossible becoming possible. It was his soul's destiny and he has gone down in history for the accomplishment. Having popped that TruthBubble, 46 days later another runner also ran a mile in under 4 minutes. And today, it is a relatively regular occurrence.

When it comes to breakthroughs in the big areas of life, of your life, I think it's especially important to consider how much the creation of that new TruthBubble will also uplift, enrich, and expand others. Using the example of Roger Bannister, apparently when he crossed the finish line and the announcer said his time was three.... the roar of the crowd, of 3,000 spectators, drowned out the rest of the announcement. His time was 3 minutes 59.4 seconds. His achievement was *our* achievement. Like going to the moon, these are breakthroughs for the human race and advance the possibilities for all of us. To the extent your new TruthBubble will uplift, enrich, and positively expand the TruthBubble of others, you will have greater capacity to create it. The force of Evolutionary Love will be on your side and the cosmic winds of grace will be at your back.

In our next chapter we'll go deeper into the process of creating new TruthBubbles and see what it takes to really break free.

References and Resources

- *Experience:* **Try on a new or different belief for a day and see how it shapes your experience.** Some suggested beliefs, or Truth-Bubbles to try out:
    - ◆ Everything that happens today is a good thing that needed to happen, was supposed to happen, and serves the highest and best outcome for everyone.
    - ◆ I see love and beauty in all things, and when appropriate, share, express and reflect that love and beauty back to where I see it.

- ◆ Everything is a miracle that I see, appreciate, and share.
- ◆ Make up your own perfect belief to try on for a day and see what happens.

- *Experience*: **3 minutes of silence,** just breathing. On the in breath say to yourself "Just," on the outbreath say to yourself "This." Or, on the in breath say to yourself "I am" and on the outbreath say to yourself "Enough."

- *Read*: **The Silent Pulse – A Search for the Perfect Rhythm that Exists in Each of Us, George Leonard, 2006**

  "From how the rich vibrations of music touch us emotionally to how the body and mind are made up of rhythmic waves, *The Silent Pulse* takes readers on a journey of self-discovery into the limitless possibilities of individual potential."

- *Read*: **The Yugas - Keys to Understanding Our Hidden Past, Emerging Energy Age, and Enlightened Future, Joseph Selbie and David Steinmetz, 2010**

  "With far-reaching changes happening on virtually a daily basis, many are wondering if we are due for a world-changing global shift, and what the future holds for mankind. Paramhansa Yogananda (author of the classic Autobiography of a Yogi) and his teacher, Sri Yukteswar, offered key insights into this subject nearly a century ago. They presented a fascinating explanation of the rising and falling eras that our planet cycles through every 24,000 years. According to their teachings, we have recently passed through the low ebb in that cycle and are moving forward to a higher age—an Energy Age that will revolutionize the world. They declared that we would live in a time of great social and spiritual change, and that much of what we believed to be fixed and true—our entire way of looking at the world—would ultimately be transformed and uplifted. In *The Yugas*, Joseph Selbie and David Steinmetz present substantial and intriguing evidence from the findings of historians and scientists that demonstrate the truth of Yukteswar and Yogananda's revelations."

- *Read*: **The Future of the Body - Explorations into the Further Evolution of Human Nature, Michael Murphy, 1992**

  "In *The Future of the Body*, he presents evidence for metanormal perception, cognition, movement, vitality, and spiritual development from more than 3,000 sources. Surveying ancient and modern records in medical science, sports, anthropology, the arts, psychical research, comparative religious studies, and dozens of other disciplines, Murphy has created an encyclopedia of exceptional functioning of body, mind, and spirit. He paints a broad and convincing picture of the possibilities of further evolutionary development of human attributes. By studying metanormal abilities under a wide range of conditions, Murphy suggests that we can identify those activities that typically evoke these capacities and assemble them into a coherent program of transformative practice."

- *Read*: **Authors of the Impossible – The Paranormal and the Sacred, Jeffrey J. Kripal, 2010**

  "Most scholars dismiss research into the paranormal as pseudoscience, a frivolous pursuit for the paranoid or gullible. Even historians of religion, whose work naturally attends to events beyond the realm of empirical science, have shown scant interest in the subject. But the history of psychical phenomena, Jeffrey J. Kripal contends, is an untapped source of insight into the sacred and by tracing that history through the last two centuries of Western thought we can see its potential centrality to the critical study of religion. [Through this book] Kripal ushers the reader into a beguiling world somewhere between fact, fiction, and fraud. The cultural history of telepathy, teleportation, and UFOs; a ghostly love story; the occult dimensions of science fiction; cold war psychic espionage; galactic colonialism; and the intimate relationship between consciousness and culture all come together in Authors of the Impossible, a dazzling and profound look at how the paranormal bridges the sacred and the scientific."

- *Read*: **The Tao of Leadership – Leadership Strategies for a New Age, John Heider, 1985 (updated 2015)**

  "This bestselling masterpiece of practical philosophy will guide you to enhanced interpersonal relationships and the cultivation of enduring leadership qualities. Heider provides simplest and clearest advice on how to be the very best kind of leader: be faithful, trust the process, pay attention, and inspire others to become their own leaders. The Tao of Leadership is a blend of practical insight and profound wisdom, offering inspiration and advice."

- *Read*: **The Intelligent Heart – Transform Your Life with the Laws of Love, David McArthur and Bruce McArthur, 1997 (updated 2018)**

  "This book teaches the universal spiritual laws that transform our lives. It reveals the presence of your heart's intelligence and how to access it. This unique, powerful domain of intelligence, different from your brain, is there to guide you to meet your life's challenges with effectiveness and wisdom."

- *Watch*: **Bashar, channeled by Darryl Anka, www.Bashar.org**

  "Bashar is a non-physical being, a friend from the future who has spoken for the past 37 years through channel Darryl Anka. He has brought through a wave of new information that clearly explains in detail how the universe works, and how each person creates the reality they experience. Over the years, thousands of individuals have had the opportunity to apply these principles, and see that they really work to change their lives and create the reality that they desire. Overwhelmingly the response is 'This works!'"

- *Read*: **The Masters of Limitation – An ET's Observations of Earth, by Darryl Anka as dictated by Bashar, 2020**
  "This book offers not only a unique perspective of human society and our place in the universe, but also gifts us with life-changing information that can profoundly alter our view of reality."

Chapter 8

Going Deeper

"Creating a society which encourages unlimited freedom is what we must all focus on now, to the exclusion of all else!"

– GREGG EISENBERG, LETTING GO IS ALL WE HAVE TO HOLD ONTO

"The wound is the place where the light enters you."

– RUMI

Your Path is Unique

Remember, your path of practice, the practice of creating your Truth-Bubbles, will be unique. Don't *believe* anything I say in this book. Take what is here and try it out for yourself. Run the experiments in your own life and see what does and does not work for you. You may need to walk slowly into this practice and take some tiny little baby steps, or you may be ready to wizard some amazing miraculous new TruthBubbles that totally transform your life. You are your own authority, you are the captain of your ship, you get to say where you are sailing and how it will be done.

The best teachers in life will always turn you toward yourself and affirm that you have everything you need, you are enough, and you are the answer you are looking for. Be very wary of any teacher who says they have or know the "Truth" with a capital "T." They may know what's true with a capital "T" for *themselves*, how-ever to claim they know what's true for everyone and for all time is a claim no one can make.

> The best teachers in life will always turn you toward yourself and affirm that you have everything you need, you are enough, and you are the answer you are looking for.

Hold Your TruthBubbles Lightly and Maintain Your Sense of Humor

I can offer some suggestions, insights, and perhaps some guidance based on what has worked for me, but I am not telling you "how this works" with any absolute authority. That would be simply creating a new Truth-Bubble and telling you to live into it. I've had to be very aware and careful as I wrote this book to not create a new TruthBubble to replace the ones that cur-rently exist. In some ways I don't think there is any way around that; to point out and create anything is to point out and create a TruthBubble. However, if we are aware of it, perhaps we can hold our TruthBubbles lightly and remain open to discovery. To ascertain the value of a TruthBubble we might ask "Does the adoption of the TruthBubble increase joy, love, and beauty for

> Does the adoption of the TruthBubble increase joy, love, and beauty for ourselves and everyone on the planet?" If the answer is yes, it just may be a TruthBubble worthy of living into.

ourselves and everyone on the planet?" If the answer is yes, it just may be a TruthBubble worthy of living into.

And, let's maintain our sense of humor. I agree with those who say that once you lose your sense of humor you are really screwed! Our sense of humor keeps us sane. We often lose our sense of humor when things get very challenging. While you may have some TruthBubbles operating in your life that are creating pain and suffering, I encourage you to hold, especially those, lightly. Being able to see them as a TruthBubble and not take them so seriously will be your first step toward their release.

It's not about avoiding or making fun of what is very challenging and hard to accept, it's about bringing some light to those darker areas of our lives so we can enter into them more easily and change them from the inside out. Approach your practice of creating new TruthBubbles with commitment, focus, intention, an open heart, committed but not attached, and with a good sense of humor. It will be a lot more fun that way – and effective!

Putting Down the Shield, Removing Armor

Going back to Chapter 1, *The Water We Swim In*, some of the more challenging TruthBubbles to transform are those created by us during our process of domestication. Those TruthBubbles about how reality is, have been on autopilot for a long time and we've forgotten we created them. A lot of what is operating in our unconscious mind has been created in response to childhood experiences, especially difficult and traumatic ones. Because of these experiences we created defense mechanisms in our minds to keep us safe and prevent overwhelming emotions that at that time we had no capacity to deal with. Even as adults, strong emotions can be challenging to deal with. No wonder we keep them suppressed and out of site.

However, just because they are suppressed and out of our "conscious awareness" does not mean they are gone – oh no – they are very present, and in many ways our entire lives are managed by and around those trigger points. We keep our armor and defense shields up, trying to protect us and keep us safe. And while they once worked magic for us, they are now wreaking havoc for us. It's our armor and our shields that have become limiting TruthBubbles that we have outgrown. Once again, we find we are like the elephant and the fleas.

> To create substantially new TruthBubbles we must address the unconscious part of ourselves that is creating our realities on autopilot.

Working with the Unconscious Mind

To create substantially new TruthBubbles we must address the unconscious part of ourselves that is creating our realities on autopilot. When healed, when transformed, whole new and wonderful TruthBubbles can emerge for us.

> "Until you make the unconscious conscious, it will direct your life and you will call it fate."
>
> - CARL JUNG

Because these parts of ourselves are unconscious, they are more difficult to see and work with. However, fortunately, many people have created pathways and processes for us to heal these wounds and help us be more positive and creative in our lives. In fact, the various ways for healing ourselves is expanding more and more every day. There is such a need for it since so much of our individual and collective suffering and violence is sourced from these unconscious wounds. Collectively we have a lot of healing to do to move through and beyond the violence we do each day to ourselves and others.

Who Are You to Poo Poo the Path?

Most of the healing paths and processes are challenging, sacred, and very important work. Because it can be challenging and scary, many people avoid this kind of work. They may even say it's not necessary, poo poo it, and think it's a bunch of new age bullshit. In truth, the people saying this are more than likely the ones who need it the most. They may be suffering in silence and have resigned themselves to their suffering (that's just the way it is, get over it), and are unfortunately, propagating their wounding out onto others.

Also, it's quite likely those who poo poo the work are the ones most afraid to embark on it. And rightfully so, I don't think anyone approaches this work without some kind of fear and trepidation. Most people who actually do the work are those that are suffering the most. These are people that can't take it anymore and are looking for a way out, a way to relieve the suffering and move forward in their lives.

It could also be that those who avoid this work, or don't understand it, may not be suffering as much. Perhaps they have created coping mechanisms that are "working" for them in our society. Maybe their particular form of shield and defense mechanisms have created some level of worldly success and wealth or fame for them, so they think "hey, I'm fine." When in reality they are not fine and are not satisfied, they're just afraid to admit it, since they, especially those that are successful and put onto a pedestal, are supposed to be happy and fine.

There are plenty of examples of those who have "made it" who suffer greatly and commit suicide not knowing there are other options for moving forward. They had bought our society's myth that becoming successful in a material sense will create happiness. Studies have shown that once you are above the poverty line when it comes to money, the incremental amount of happiness provided by more money is small. Once your basic needs are met for warmth, shelter, food, and clothing, additional money buys you very little in the way of happiness. And, as I like to say, you become "possessed by your possessions" – keeping and managing your money and stuff becomes the thing you have to do.

Climbing the Mountain One Step at a Time

The path of healing these wounds and freeing ourselves from their influence is usually not a "one and done" experience, as much as we would like it to be that way. It's like climbing a mountain in a spiral fashion. You'll heal an aspect and take in a whole new view, then as you journey around and upwards you come around again to that same area of your life. You get triggered in some way and think "WTF? I thought I healed that?!!" Well, you did, at some level, and now it's time to go deeper. You're at a new level in your life, you have climbed further up the mountain, and a new level of healing is required for your journey to continue.

So, don't despair if some of the same issues and challenges keep popping up. It's possible that you're not engaging the right modalities for you to heal, however, if you have felt a healing in the past around a wound or trauma, then it's more likely that you're just going deeper to new levels of healing and freedom. Doing this very important and sacred work will change your vibration and provide you access to new TruthBubbles.

The Only Way Out is Through

On this healing path I've found there are no shortcuts, there is no by-passing the process. The only way out is through. Meaning, you have to feel the pain in the body itself. You cannot simply "think" your way to healing. Because we energetically store our wounds and traumas in our actual body, you must be willing to access, re-experience, and bring alive that energetic feeling in your body.

Another way of saying this is you must feel it to heal it. This has been totally true in my experience and the processes that work best will facilitate this level of feeling engagement. So, when doing any of these processes, if it is working you will feel the wound in you, you will re-experience the trauma but this time you will be consciously experiencing it and engaged in a process to help you see it, embrace it, welcome and even love it. And, eventually integrate it back into your conscious awareness. You will have it rather than it having you. You will love all parts of yourself back together again so you are more whole, free, and no longer at effect of these hidden energy patterns still trying to protect you.

> Because we energetically store our wounds and traumas in our actual body, you must be willing to access, re-experience, and bring alive that energetic feeling in your body.

So, allow the discomfort, allow the tears, allow even the fears of any kind to be felt, to flow, and to move through and out. It's a cleansing, a clearing, and it's the way to more freedom and access to the TruthBubbles you really want of more safety, love, and beauty in the world.

The Bottom Line – Processes to Engage

Driven by my suffering and desire for more freedom, creativity and self-expression, I've engaged many forms and processes for healing; from the very simple and affordable to the incredibly complex and expensive. I've listed below things I've engaged and found helpful. I have loosely organized and listed them starting with the more simple, affordable, less time-consuming processes on up to the more complex, pricier and more time consuming.

There may be some correlation with these criteria to the power and effectiveness of a process, but not necessarily so. Simple, self-administered processes can provide profound healing if you're ready for it. This is by no means a complete list, and the things that will work for you may not be on it. Follow your intuition with where to start and go from there:

Self-administered processes for reflection and healing

- **Simple journaling –** just allowing your thoughts and feelings to flow in a free form fashion onto a page can be cathartic. It's a form of identifying and declaring what's swimming around in you causing stress. By identifying and declaring these thoughts and feelings you can see them more clearly, find new ways forward, and if you're ready, "let that shit go."
- **Byron Katie's The Work:** www.TheWork.com
"As we do The Work of Byron Katie, not only do we remain alert to our stressful thoughts—the ones that cause all the anger, sadness, and frustration in our world—but we question them, and through that questioning the thoughts lose their power over us. Great spiritual texts describe the what—what it means to be free.

The Work is the how. It shows you exactly how to identify and question any thought that would keep you from that freedom."

- **The Seven Step Expansion Process:** From Sad to Glad – 7 Steps to Facing Change with Love and Power, Janet Bray Attwood and Chris Attwood. www.ThePassionTest.com/from-sad-to-glad

  "While the 7-step Expansion Process emerged from the challenges of facing drastic change in the nature of their relationship, Janet and Chris have demonstrated that this simple process is equally effective for facing change in business, in health, in location or any other upheaval which life may throw at us."

- **Marc Allen's Core Belief Process:** The Greatest Secret of All – Simple Steps to Abundance, Fulfillment, and a Life Well Lived, 2011

  "It is essential to become aware of the beliefs we carry with us, and see how much they affect every moment of our lives. Even just becoming aware of these beliefs is a great step toward letting them go, if we wish, or changing them into much more powerful, positive beliefs."

- **Frank Lobsiger's Welcoming Process:** The Art of SelfLove – Loving Yourself is the Key to Happiness. www.TheArtofSelfLove.com

  "Through Frank's easy-to-follow 3-step Welcoming- Process™, you will learn how to relate to yourself in a conscious and loving way, no matter the circumstances."

- **Robert Scheinfeld's The Process:** Busting Loose from the Business Game – Mind Blowing Strategies for Recreating Yourself, Your Team, Your Customers, Your Business, and Everything in Between, 2009

  "Power is hidden inside *all* the illusions you experience while playing The Human Game. However, the greatest amount of power, the biggest lies, and the biggest illusions are located where you feel discomfort." Apply the five steps of The Process anytime you feel discomfort. "As you expand more and more, and collapse more and more limiting patterns in The Field, the power, wisdom, abundance, and True Joy that are your natural state start shining through more and more, and your life and business become more and more miraculous."

- **The Sedona Method:** www.Sedona.com

  "The Sedona Method is a simple, powerful, and easy-to-learn technique that shows you how to uncover your natural ability to let go of any painful or unwanted feeling in the moment. There are five ways to approach the process of releasing, and they all lead to the same result: liberating your natural ability to let go of any unwanted emotion on the spot, and allowing some of the suppressed energy in your subconscious to dissipate revealing your unlimited potential."

- **Toltec Inventory and Recapitulation Processes.** https://www.joydancer.com/book.html

  These Toltec tools are simply outlined in *The Everything Toltec Wisdom Book – A complete guide to the ancient wisdoms,* by Allan Hardman, a Toltec Master trained by don Miguel Ruiz, author of *The Four Agreements.* "The essence of recapitulation is in finding the lies in the mind's mitote, and changing them to truth. The warrior stalks the old dream with its beliefs and agreements based on fear, and releases them to reveal the natural truth of love and perfection hidden under them. Recapitulation is a detailed formal method for mining deep into the mind in search of every memory held by fear and judgement. It has freed many warriors from the prisons of their domestication."

Processes that are a bit more involved and may require a facilitator (at least initially)

- **Bill McKenna's CognoMovement Process:** www.CognoMovement.com

  "Cognomovement is a system that includes all of your senses, Auditory, Visual and Kinesthetic (movement) to create immediate change in your body, mind, and consciousness! These changes are fast and lasting! You can do it for yourself, your clients, find a practitioner or become a practitioner. You can attend classes and seminars to facilitate your massive change, releasing your natural energy and helping you create your very best life."

- **Breathwork** (e.g., Stanislav Grof's Holotropic Breathwork)
  Visit Wikipedia page for general overview and access to links: https://en.wikipedia.org/wiki/Breathwork

- **Hypnotherapy:** HCH Institute (Hypnotherapy Clearing House) – www.HypnotherapyTraining.com

- **Psychotherapy:** American Psychological Association – Understanding psychotherapy and how it works, https://www.apa.org/topics/psychotherapy/understanding

Processes and programs that are much more involved

- **The Landmark Forum:** www.LandmarkWorldwide.com
  "The Landmark Forum is grounded in a model of transformative learning – a way of learning that gives people an awareness of the basic structures in which they know, think, and act. From that awareness comes a fundamental shift that leaves people more fully in accord with their own possibilities and those of

others. Participants find themselves able to think and act beyond existing views and limits – in their personal and professional lives, relationships, and wider communities of interest"

- **Psychedelics:** Whether solo or in a group, the process should be done in a sacred manner and coordinated by well trained and experienced facilitators

  - ◆ **MAPS – Multidisciplinary Association for Psychedelic Studies**, www.MAPS.org

    MAPS is a leader in psychedelic research. Since 1986, MAPS has been on a mission to create safe, legal, and beneficial opportunities for psychedelics in medicine and society.

  - ◆ **San Francisco Psychedelic Society** - https://psychedelicsocietysf.org

    A 501(c)(3) non-profit dedicated to helping individuals, and the global community, unlock the healing and transformative potential of psychedelics while seeking to honor their indigenous lineages.

  - ◆ **Rythmia Life Advancement Center** – www.Rythmia.com

    Rythmia is a medically-licensed everything-included wellness center and resort in Guanacaste, Costa Rica. They offer and integrate plant medicine, yoga, breathwork, meditation, transformational workshops designed by Michael Bernard Beckwith, spa and massage services, and organic food.

Long-term paths of practice for ongoing maintenance and continual growth and development:

- **Integral Transformative Practice** – www.ITP-International.org
  Integral Transformative Practice® is a roadmap for your evolutionary

unfolding in body, mind, heart and soul. Inspired by ancient and contemporary wisdom and supported by a deeply connected community, ITP brings balance, vitality, purpose and joy into your life. As you transform yourself, you transform the world.

- **HearthMath®** – www.HeartMath.com
  Founded in 1991 by Doc Childre, HeartMath has developed a system of effective, scientifically based tools and technologies to bridge the intuitive connection between heart and mind and deepen our connection with the hearts of others.

- **Meditation** - https://www.mindful.org/how-to-meditate/

- **Life Coaching** – www.CoachingFederation.org
  Hiring a professionally trained and certified coach as a co-creative partner can be incredibly powerful for moving one's life forward in new directions and dimensions. For 25 years the International Coaching Federation (ICF) has been leading the way and setting high standards for this profession.

One final note on engaging processes and various practices. Have you ever noticed that some things work for some people but not for others? Why is that? Why is it that a process, practice or modality doesn't work on all people all the time? Well, there are many different ways you can interpret or explain this, and note that every way will be a TruthBubble. A TruthBubble to explain this that I have found helpful was presented by Bashar (remember from Chapter 7 Bashar is the off-planet entity channeled by the living man named Darryl Anka). Bashar explains this phenomenon of some things working for

> Permission slips are things in our life that allow us to access and engage our infinite creative power.

some people but not for others with a concept he calls "Permission Slips." Permission slips are things in our life that allow us to access and engage our infinite creative power. As many teachers and healers will say (at least the good ones) "I am not healing you. You are healing yourself." We could say the healer is "the permission slip" the client needed to access their own healing capacities and heal themselves. Some people need doctors in white coats in a clinic, others need shamans on the Amazon river. Some people respond to hypnotherapy, while others need psychotherapy. All of these things are examples of permission slips that give us permission to create whatever it is we are wanting to create in our lives. We need to experiment and explore to find the unique permission slips that work for us.

Chapter 9

Worlds Collide

"I like to learn from all people, but especially
those that agree with me."

– Gregg Eisenberg, Letting Go Is All We Have to Hold Onto

"Democracy in its simplest form of sharing power, listening, and
gathering information, is the only sustainable form of governing
ourselves, because no one likes being told what to do by others."

– Arnold Mindell, Psychologist and Writer

Roger, won't this approach of everyone living in their own TruthBubbles lead to total chaos and anarchy as everyone becomes selfishly focused on creating and having their own TruthBubbles? Good question! I'm glad you asked. Well, the truth is, everybody is *already* living in and creating their own TruthBubbles, they just don't know it! And look at what kind of a world that is creating for us.

What I'm trying to do here is wake us up to the fact we each live in a reality and an experience that is unique to us. Once we realize there are 7 billion plus different realities on the planet, we can stop trying to convince everybody that our particular TruthBubble is the right one. We can have our TruthBubble with no need for anyone else to believe in it. This is our first step toward **peace** – not chaos. What we have now, due to the unconscious creation of default TruthBubbles being imposed on others, is relative chaos.

Once you are free to have *your own* truth, you can then let others have *their own* truth too. You don't need to manipulate them, control them, or kill them, so that you can have the Truth-Bubble you want. This removes a lot of fear-based pain and suffering inflicted in our world spent defending and promoting TruthBubbles as a reality everyone must believe in for it to be true. This saves a lot

> Once you are free to have *your own* truth, you can then let others have *their own* truth too.

of time and effort – no need to go on crusade converting people to your TruthBubble. So, what this actually leads to first, is a peaceful experience of each person rightfully living in their own TruthBubble and allowing everyone else to do the same.

This is the first step toward peace and harmony – allowing everyone to have their TruthBubble without any need to change them so we can be safe and loved. My safety and my love, as we saw in Chapter 5, *The Source of Love*, comes from Source itself. I don't need others to believe what I believe to get my safety and love. I have access to an infinite supply already, in fact I have so much, I have some for others if they want it.

With that said, it's clear we live in a world with lots of other people. And there is a reason it's been said "Hell is other people." As we have seen, hell is readily available. The question is, how do we create heaven with these other people? As human beings we are social creatures; we want and need to interact, collaborate, and ultimately co-create with other people. How do we do this most effectively and efficiently?

When TruthBubbles Intersect

Using the concept of TruthBubbles, we can look at various scenarios we'll experience when interacting with other people and *their* personal TruthBubbles. Lots has been said about this terrain under various titles like cooperation, collaboration, teamwork, communication, parenting, leadership, negotiation, persuasion, influencing, non-violent communication, listening, etc. All of these areas of human experience deal with intersecting TruthBubbles between people. When TruthBubbles intersect we have basically three possible scenarios:

1. TruthBubbles totally overlap – there is complete and total agreement on how the world or reality is, the truth of something,
2. TruthBubbles partially overlap – there is some agreement on how the world or reality is, the truth of something, and
3. TruthBubbles have no overlap – there is no agreement, and potentially there is disagreement, on how the world or reality is and the truth of something.

The Approach

First, it's important to get clear on your intention. I'm going to assume you are not interested in creating more conflict, suffering, and misery for yourself and others in the world. Therefore, our intention is to create more harmony, collaboration, connection, co-creation, teamwork, and some expanded experience of safety, love, and beauty. This is our goal, or our intended outcome. And, yes, there can be a place for "conflict." However, productive conflict is the type that is held in a container of love, with an intention of creating more harmony, collaboration and teamwork *through* the conflict. Without that clear intention and container, conflict will typically result in more separation and suffering.

It's very important to keep in mind our goal, or intention, and be clear *where we are coming from*. Because as we've seen, if we're coming from a fear-based need for safety and love, if we are not feeling safe or loved, then our goal or desired outcome is by default to get our needs for safety and love met. That is what we will be trying to "get" from the other people. But if we are already grounded in love, and have

> **It's very important to keep in mind our goal, or intention, and be clear *where we are coming from*.**

all the safety and love we need, we are able to *offer* that to others, and our desire is not to "get that from others" but offer it so we can experience an expanded state of safety and love *with* others. And, maybe even create more and more safety and love in the world for more and more people. Such that, eventually, everyone's needs for safety and love are met. Now we're living in heaven on earth!

So, the first thing when engaging other people, other TruthBubbles, is to clarify your love-based intention and ensure you are grounded in and coming from your source, your source of safety and love. That is step one. The second is to recognize that you, yourself, are by the very fact you are alive, living in a TruthBubble. Since you know you are living in a TruthBubble, you hold your beliefs and ways of seeing the world lightly. And, because of that, you are free in your exploration of worldviews and other TruthBubbles. You are free to open up to and listen to and engage the worldviews and TruthBubbles of others.

Now others, unless they've read this book, will probably not relate to their worldview or ways of seeing reality as a TruthBubble. They will probably relate to it as the truth, since it is in fact what they are experiencing, or have experienced. Even If they don't relate to their perspective as the truth, they probably believe there is "a truth" out there to be known and that it's just a matter of most accurately finding it. This is important to be aware of. They may be attached to their TruthBubble, or attached to "a reality out there," and unwilling to look at other ways of seeing things. Especially if they believe their needs for safety and love are dependent upon it.

An enemy is a stranger who's story you haven't heard.

To summarize, as we engage other TruthBubbles, we are 1) clear on our intention to create more safety, love, and beauty in the world, 2) grounded in our own source of safety and love, 3) aware that we ourselves are living in a TruthBubble, and 4) aware that others may be understandably attached to their views. From here, now we can begin to explore the TruthBubbles of others.

Get Curious

The next thing I recommend you do is get curious. Get genuinely curious in how this other person or people, see the world. See if you can discover their TruthBubble they are living in. How do you do this? By asking questions. Ask the questions that help you, and them, see the worldview, the perspective, the beliefs, the values, they are holding that make up their TruthBubble.

It's always better to be interested in others and where they are coming from vs. putting your worldview and "how you see things" out there first. Be interested in others, give them some love by honoring them and their worldview by really listening. Remember, an enemy is a stranger whose story you have not heard. Work to hear their story. What is their life experience that is informing and creating their worldview, their TruthBubbles? Seek first to understand before seeking to be understood. Ask them questions and then listen intently to their responses. As you listen to what they are saying you will begin to see where

> It's always better to be interested in others and where they are coming from vs. putting your worldview and "how you see things" out there first.

your TruthBubble and their TruthBubble(s) exist and how much, if any, overlap there is. Knowing this will help you discern how best to move forward.

Extending Compassion

Another incredibly important perspective to maintain and offer "the other" is compassion. They believe and hold the worldview or TruthBubble they're in for a *reason*. And that reason, they believe, is there to serve them. The TruthBubbles of others may look totally insane to us, from our perspective, but that is only because we are living in our own TruthBubble that sees theirs as insane. They don't see their TruthBubble as insane, they see it as totally logical given the experiences they have had and are having and what they are now trying to get or create. So, we must extend compassion to them. Even if, and perhaps especially if, they are engaged in violence of some kind – mental, emotional, or physical.

Violence is exerting your will over another by using force. Why would someone exert their will over another using force? Because they are afraid. They are rooted in and coming from fear. They are not grounded in and coming from their infinite source of safety and love. And because they are rooted in and coming from fear, they believe, and they even experience, that the only way they can be safe and loved is to control and manipulate the world, which might include you in some way shape or form. As we saw, when coming from the fear-based, separate sense of self, one experiences limitation and scarcity; there is only one pie and I gotta get my piece, or the whole pie if I can.

TruthBubbles created in fear are just as real as those created in love. And because they are created in fear, they are very scary! It sucks to live in TruthBubbles created from fear because they perpetuate more fear, and create experiences of fear, and lead to thoughts, feelings, and actions that are designed to alleviate the experienced fear. However, those thoughts, feelings, and actions never alleviate the fear. Why? Because actions sourced from fear beget more fear. Hence, the most appropriate response when encountering TruthBubbles based in fear, is compassion. These people need the *most* love and compassion since they are not having an experience of that at all. Therefore, our best and most appropriate move is to come from and extend compassion. This opens up the communication channels, softens our heart, and by extension begins to soften theirs too.

The typical response to fear-based TruthBubbles is usually some sort of automatic human response based in survival: fight, flight, or freeze. In some cases where your life is literally threatened these responses are probably appropriate. However, most of the "threats" we experience in our everyday lives are not directly life threatening. Nonetheless, if you are rooted in fear, and coming from fear, and therefore lacking in safety and love, your response to another's fear-based TruthBubble will be one of these automatic defense and survival responses. These responses may perpetuate your survival – maybe – but they will not evolve the situation to one of more peace, harmony, love and safety. Remember our goal?

We want to be grounded in our own source of safety and love; offering it to others, not seeking it from them. And, extending compassion for whatever their experience or TruthBubble is. From here we can fully allow them to have and live in their TruthBubble. We are not trying to take their truth away, and because we are not here to take that away we are less of a threat to them. Initially, we are just trying to understand, to see where *they* stand. What do they believe, why do they believe that, what is their intention and desired outcome? We are in exploratory dialogue coming from compassion, safety, and love.

> We want to be grounded in our own source of safety and love; offering it to others, not seeking it from them.

Now, very often, especially if someone is afraid and they are creating a certain TruthBubble out of their need for safety and love, they will be trying to change *your* TruthBubble. This happens because they think that meeting their needs for safety and love requires *you* to believe and affirm what *they* believe and affirm. They need your worldview to agree with theirs, because if it doesn't, then their strategy for getting the safety and love they perceive they need is threatened. Now *you* are a threat to their ability to get the safety and love they believe they need.

This is why it is so important to be coming from your own infinite source of safety and love when engaging fear-based TruthBubbles. As Gandhi is famous for saying "You must be the change you are seeking in the world." If you resort to violence, to some form of attack on their Truth-Bubble, you will not be able to achieve the greater peace, love, harmony, connection and collaboration you are seeking. Remember, as Gandhi is also famous for having said, "An eye for an eye makes us both blind."

I am not saying this is easy, it is not. If your TruthBubble, even if created from your infinite source of safety and love, does not align with the fear-based TruthBubble of another, they will likely attack you, or at least your TruthBubble. You must be able to withstand this attack without fighting back. Fighting war with more war only creates more war. You must hold the higher ground and invite them up to it. This is sacred work. It is the path of evolutionary love and moves all of humanity forward.

> "You never change things by fighting the existing reality. To change something, build a new model that makes the existing model obsolete."
>
> -R. BUCKMINSTER FULLER

When being attacked for not believing and seeing the world the same way someone else sees it you will likely experience a fair amount of tension in the conversation. Remember, the other person believes their survival is at stake so they will likely be pretty intense about their worldview and perspective. They are attached to it because the safety and love they need (and they do need it) is dependent on their TruthBubble. If you are seeing the world in a different way, if you are getting your safety and love met in a different way, one that they cannot understand or believe they cannot access, then they will, they must, convince you that your way is ridiculous and their way is the only way. Hence you will be attacked, verbally, mentally, emotionally and maybe physically.

TruthBubbles As Identity

Another thing to be aware of is most people have their worldview and *who they are* wrapped up as one. The way they see the world, the TruthBubbles they live in, is their identity. They are identified with their

TruthBubbles for their very existence. Hence, if their TruthBubble is threatened, they literally believe and experience they themselves, their very existence, is threatened. This of course elevates the need to be right and for their TruthBubbles to be the one that survives, the one that wins, since their existence depends on it. This further emphasizes why compassion is a very important mindset to adopt when interacting with people for whom this is true.

Of course, we can totally understand this. We've all been there, we can relate. We ourselves are living in a TruthBubble when we engage them, no matter how loving and open. We are hopefully grounded in our infinite source of safety and love, a bit freer when it comes to how we hold our own TruthBubbles, and hopefully more able to listen and offer the safety and love, even if just a vibration of possibility, they are seeking.

Lessons From Plant Medicine

I had an experience of my worldview and "who I thought I was" being confronted and challenged in my first ever ayahuasca ceremony. After my very first cup I was sitting upright for about 30 minutes to allow the medicine to sink into my stomach. When I started seeing energy matrices and interesting geometric forms being overlayed on the ceremonial maloca I was in, I knew the medicine was taking effect. I laid down and closed my eyes.

It wasn't long before I began totally slipping into an entirely different reality. I experienced a moment of terror as my worldview, the everyday waking reality and how I put my world together, was being flipped on its head and ultimately completely dismantled. It was, quite frankly, very scary, and I had a momentary thought that this was too much for me, that I had "gotten in over my head" and was not going to be able to deal with it.

Well, it's true, I *was* in over my head! The rational, attached, linear, survival-oriented, mechanistic part of myself was *not* going to be able to deal with this. I had to let go of that TruthBubble, that way of seeing and being in the world, and allow a whole new way to emerge. By softening my body, by breathing deeply, by affirming a position of gratefulness, by allowing and embracing any and all experiences arising, I found a new way to navigate in this strange new world; one based on surrender rather than control, one based on curiosity, openness, and discovery, rather than expectation and predictability.

Interestingly as I journeyed further into the experience, Mother Ayahuasca, as she is called, offered me some insight and guidance on this TruthBubble work that had been coming through me since the release of my first book, *NexGen Human*. She said, "Roger, know that worldviews are at the center of one's experience, how one makes up and makes sense of the world is equal to who one believes they actually are. By changing worldviews (TruthBubbles) you are literally changing who a person actually is. This is important and very sacred work, and should be done with the highest levels of respect and compassion. People have constructed their TruthBubbles over entire lives. Each day and every moment, they are living into and through their TruthBubbles. Even if they are suffering in those TruthBubbles, it is who they know themselves to be. Approach this work cautiously, with reverence for the miracle that it is that humans can construct reality in this way. Move gently, with love, and do your work to offer new possibilities, new pathways, and whole new worlds, to people that are ready for them."

This message from Mother Ayahuasca was so powerful for me *because* I had earlier in that very same journey, viscerally experienced exactly what she was talking about. It was terrifying to have my worldview ripped out from underneath me. And it did feel like a ripping out since it came on so quickly as I rapidly descended into a whole new world requiring a whole new worldview. She gave me that experience of a total worldview change, and how scary and disorienting it can be, and then gently shared with me why this is such sacred work and why it's so important for me to approach it with great reverence, compassion, understanding, and love.

This advice from Mother Ayahuasca I offer to you. Know that the very act of creating a TruthBubble is a miracle. Hold this capacity we have as humans incredibly sacred. Even if the TruthBubbles being created are causing pain and suffering, the mechanism behind it is miraculous and sacred. Approach your own creating and shifting of your *own* TruthBubbles with compassion. Honor the ones you've been living in and release them with great appreciation for whatever level of service and safety to your life they have provided.

Know and respect that it can be incredibly scary and challenging to let go of a TruthBubble and move toward and into a whole new TruthBubble, because at the core of this process is our very experience of self. Our TruthBubbles are who we believe we are. They are our very powerful sense-making tools in a world of pure energy. And as you engage the TruthBubbles of others, offer them the same reverence, respect and compassion for

> Our TruthBubbles are who we believe we are. They are our very powerful sense-making tools in a world of pure energy.

their TruthBubbles, the journeys they've been on to construct them, and the challenge it is to navigate into and create new ones. You can be that light of possibility, of hope for a new experience, of hope for literally a whole new world. Through your own practice of navigating and creating new TruthBubbles and whole new worlds of experience for yourself, you can role model and offer that to others. It is a divine and sacred work, and it is at the very core of human existence and experience.

Or is it?

References and Resources

- *Reflect*: What do you think is the most challenging part of engaging another person that has a worldview or TruthBubble that is very different from your own? How might you best address that challenge?

- *Read*: **A Greater Democracy Day by Day, Sally Mahé and Kathy Covert, 2004**

  "This unique collection of ideas about democracy is meant to lift our spirits and remind us that there is power in our hearts to create the world we want for coming generations. Our intention in gathering these ideas is to offer a simple gift to good-hearted people in the United States and all over the world. These ideas are given to remind us of what is possible and convince us that we, the people, all of us, make a difference that counts. I hope the diverse voices in this book inspire each of us to take actions that bring beauty, dignity, justice, and healing to the world. We can do it. Now is the time."

- *Read*: **Conversations Worth Having – Using Appreciative Inquiry to Fuel Productive and Meaningful Engagement, Jackie Stavros and Cherrie Torres, 2018 (second edition 2021)**

"The practices and principles originate from the work of David Cooperrider on Appreciative Inquiry, one of the most widely used approaches for fostering positive change in organizations and communities. The two practices – positive framing and asking generative questions – can to turn any conversation into one worth having."

- *Read*: **The Surrender Experiment – My Journey into Life's Perfection, Michael A. Singer, 2015**

"Michael A. Singer, author of The Untethered Soul, tells the extraordinary story of what happened when, after a deep spiritual awakening, he decided to let go of his personal preferences and simply let life call the shots. As Singer takes you on this great experiment and journey into life's perfection, the events that transpire will both challenge your deepest assumptions about life and inspire you to look at your own life in a radically different way."

- *Read*: **Busting Loose from the Business Game – Robert Scheinfeld, 2009**

"You learned 'the rules' and you've been faithful to them, thinking you can win. But you can't really win The Business Game, because it's *designed* to be unwinnable – that is, as long as you play by the rules you were taught. The only way to truly win is to bust loose from the 'old' game and start playing a new game with a new set of rules. This book helps you discover who you really are, what you're really capable of, and how you can tap new sources of power, wisdom, and abundance to radically transform your experience in business. When you bust loose from the old game, you'll suddenly be playing a new game."

- *Watch*: The Medicine – Can an Ancient Amazonian Plant Medicine Help Heal Mankind? www.TheMedicineDocumentary. com

"The Medicine reveals the hidden mysteries of one of nature's most powerful and controversial healing remedies- Ayahuasca. It is a documentary about Amazonian shamanism, introducing Taita Juanito Guerillmo Chindoy Chindoy, both a teacher and student of the sacred plant medicine. As Ayahuasca gains popularity in the West, the film explores the science as well as the lore behind the plant and why it is used to heal. It follows former NFL Safety, Kerry Rhodes, and actress, AnnaLynne McCord, as they drink with the Taita experiencing Ayahuasca for the first time - in its true tradition. Humanity faces an unprecedented rise in addiction, insecurity and disease - perhaps the cure does lie within the arms of Mother Nature."

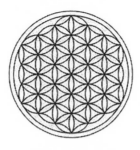

Chapter 10

Beyond the Bubbles – Going Beyond Belief

"After feeling connected with the Universe for so long, I'm looking to rent a one-room studio for a while."

– GREGG EISENBERG, LETTING GO IS ALL WE HAVE TO HOLD ONTO

"Dig as deep as you will, you will never come to a thing called Tao or God. Tao is not a thing. Tao is a principle or law. Tao means how. All things behave according to Tao, but Tao does not behave. Tao is never an object or a process. Tao is the law of all things, of all events. Tao is the common ground of all creation."

JOHN HEIDER, THE TAO OF LEADERSHIP

TruthBubbles are indeed very powerful. Worlds literally rise and fall within them. Our experience is generated through and as them. But is it who and what we are? Are we nothing but a collection of Truthbubbles? It seems that is the case. You cannot be in this world without some kind of TruthBubble. Even if your TruthBubble is that there is no TruthBubble, or that you are not a TruthBubble, you are living in a TruthBubble. It seems there is no escape – similar to the old saying "if you choose not to decide, you still have made a choice."

But TruthBubbles live in the world of *beliefs*, in *this* reality of experience. Some call this reality duality, it's a world of opposites. Nothing in our world can exist without its opposite. When you pick up one end of a stick you also, by definition, pick up the other end. Hot is only hot relative to its opposite cold.

We could also argue that we live in a world of continuums. That it's only a perception that something is the opposite of one thing. For example, is hate the opposite of love? Or is it simply the absence of love on the continuum of love itself? From this perspective, love is all that exists, and its opposite is not hate, its simply the absence of love. Either way, the *something* is defined by its existence or non-existence, and we are once again back in the world of duality.

My question to you is "what's beyond the world of duality?" What's beyond the world of things and no things? What's beyond this world we experience where we assemble and disassemble TruthBubbles? Another way of asking this might be "What is it upon or in that a TruthBubble is created and experienced?" What is the medium for experience itself? *In what* are the worlds created by TruthBubbles

> We can go beyond the TruthBubbles themselves and the game of creating new ones.

rising and falling? By exploring these questions and coming to some kind of insight, there is a new freedom to be had. We can go beyond the TruthBubbles themselves and the game of creating new ones. Since TruthBubbles are created by beliefs, in this inquiry and exploration we are literally going beyond beliefs. What's there?

There are a number of ways to explore this question and this new terrain. Meditation is one of them. I have been engaged in a committed meditation practice for more than 20 years; I love meditation. In meditation I experience being whole and complete, with nothing missing. I am completely fulfilled with no needs whatsoever. There is nowhere to go, nowhere to be, and nothing to do. The experience is complete in and of itself. AND on this whole and complete canvas, things rise and fall – of their own accord. Thoughts arise and fall, feelings arise and fall, sounds arise and fall. These are mini-TruthBubbles rising and falling.

Experiencing a thought is itself based in beliefs. I "believe" I am experiencing a thing called a thought. I have named this experience and it becomes a thing. I have also named feelings; I call the experience feelings and that is the experience I then believe I am having. However, what these thoughts and feelings, these beliefs and experiences, are rising and falling in, is what I am pointing toward. Ultimately it cannot be named, for to name it creates belief and belief creates a TruthBubble and very quickly we are no longer on point, we are back in the world of duality.

This is nothing new, seekers and sages have known this for ages. However, there is still value in distinguishing this place, this experience, that is unique and distinct from the TruthBubbles of ordinary existence. By distinguishing this place, and having some actual experience of its existence, of its reality, we become even more capable to experience and create TruthBubbles. When we are connected to the place from which they both rise and fall, we are truly free.

We can arrive at this place through a meditation practice. Some call it oneness, or nondual, or awareness itself. It's the place where everything is one, there is no duality. Duality rises in and from this oneness. The world of things, the world of TruthBubbles, rises in and on and through this nondual oneness or awareness. When we arrive there, we have gone beyond belief, we are located at the source of beliefs themselves, the point of creation itself.

I arrived at this place on one of my ayahuasca experiences. During this particular journey I had been experiencing an up and down roller coaster ride of joyful ecstatic experiences and terrifying dark experiences. I was noticing my rational mind trying to navigate and manage the experiences and as soon as I thought I had found the secret to holding myself (whatever "myself" was at that time) in a joyful ecstatic experience (because naturally that's where I wanted to stay), as soon as I said "aha, I got it" boom, down into the darkness I would go. It was a very humbling experience, and I came to realize that no strategy, no "keys," no recipe, was going to save me from the dark, terrifying and scary places. No strategy was going to keep me in the light, keep me in the joyful, ecstatic places that I longed to be.

As I came upon this realization, I surrendered to another level. I let go of my preference and attachment to the joyful, ecstatic experiences. By letting go of this attachment, I was free to more fully engage the dark and scary experiences. I started going into them remembering something I heard from a Buddhist teaching "Our demons wonder why we don't love them more." I started getting more curious about the dark and scary landscapes and experiences I was having. Rather than resisting and trying to make them go away,

> Our demons wonder why we don't love them more.

rather than trying to run to the light, I went into the darkness. I went in with curiosity, and eventually I evolved my presence of curiosity to one of appreciation. I came to appreciate something about these dark and scary places, whatever it was that I could appreciate.

As I continued on this roller coaster of dark and light, of fear and joy, I started to notice a deeper aspect of myself. I started to notice that which was noticing. I started to observe the observer. I started to see what was seeing. This noticer, this observer, this seer, was distinct from both the fear and joy that was being noticed, observed, and seen. In my journey the metaphor that worked for me was the observer was like the movie screen upon which the movies were being projected; upon which the scenes of fear and joy were rising and falling.

This place is beyond the risings and fallings, it just IS. It is the ground of being, of experience itself. I came to realize that at a deeper level of my existence, I am this movie screen, I am this awareness upon which Truth-Bubbles and the experiences they create, rise and fall. I am beyond any specific experience, and am the source from which and upon experience itself rises and falls.

Knowing that I definitely had a preference for the joyful light-based experiences and had less preference for the dark and scary experiences, and now knowing that I am the screen upon which these scenes rise and fall, I went a little deeper on this inquiry and asked "why do I, and why does humanity, create dark and scary experiences that apparently we don't prefer?" The answer I got was that we create dark and scary experiences for two reasons: 1) to feel alive, and 2) to test our greatness. This made sense to me, even though I could think of plenty of other ways to feel alive and test my greatness. I could see that any scary, challenging experience, would be a way for me, and for humanity, to feel alive and to potentially experience greatness.

Just take sports as a simple easy example. We make up hard and challenging scenarios to test us. In the process of "playing the game," and especially when we succeed, we feel alive and we feel our greatness. Just think of the Super Bowl and how alive and great everyone on the winning team feels. It's a totally made-up game to produce this exact experience. The thing with sports is we can see we made it up. However, when it comes to dark and scary experiences in "real" life, it can be hard, almost impossible, to see that we also made it up; that we are the creators of the experience. These dark and scary experiences run the full gamut from very personal to very global.

With the sports analogy, because we know we made it up, we also know that we can say if we wanted to "Hey, hold on a minute, let's stop this silliness and do something else." However, with other dark and scary experiences, it's not so clear that we created them and that we can stop and change them if we wanted to.

The Bottom Line - Our Journey from Fear to Love

This is the level of awareness that is possible for us as humans. That we can first awaken to our TruthBubbles *and* awaken to a reality *beyond* them. We can stop running from our dark and scary experiences, love our demons more and more, and from that place of acceptance, compassion and courage, begin creating more love-based and joyful TruthBubbles and experiences.

I believe this journey **from fear to love**, at all levels and scales, personal to global, is the most challenging and exciting journey any human, indeed humanity, can take. This journey can be our ultimate source for feeling truly alive and coming to know our greatness at the highest levels possible.

Ending Where We Began,
with An Opening

Place your hands over your heart

Bow your head toward your heart

Take three deep, slow breaths

In through the nose

Out through the mouth

Become aware of the power of your heart

Activate a feeling of appreciation and gratitude

For this moment

For your life

For the miraculous Universe inside which you exist

For the miraculous Universe which exists inside you

Breathe easy

Extend and radiate this loving energy of appreciation and gratitude out to others

ALL others

Thank you

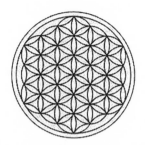

Some Example TruthBubbles

1. Beyond Belief, LLC
2. Evolutionary Panentheism
3. A Positive World Vision
4. Death and Dying

1. A TruthBubble for Business - Beyond Belief, LLC

There is a field of intelligence guiding the unfolding of the Universe. As human beings we play an important and integral role in this evolutionary unfolding, perhaps now more than ever before. As part of this unfolding, we as human beings have been given the unique gift and power of choice - we can choose our level of participation and partnership with this field in the unfolding of the Universe. At *Beyond Belief,* we have chosen to maximize our partnership with this field and be a vehicle through which others can choose and maximize their own partnership with it.

Just as everything in nature has a built-in, inherent blueprint deep within itself guiding its unfolding and life path, so does each and every human being. It is from this individual blueprint, deep within each and every one of us, that we can access, express, and live the best that life has to offer. From this deep field of energetic intelligence naturally flow the highest levels of integrity, inspiration, courage, love, peace, compassion, creativity and wisdom that humanity is capable of. When one is truly tapped into their own unique aspect of this intelligent energy, into their own individual blueprint, there is a knowing - beyond thoughts and beyond thinking - that emerges, inspiring and guiding their own right actions; actions that result in ideal outcomes for all.

Everyone has a purpose, an individual internal blueprint, they are here to create and manifest. We have bodies, minds, hearts, and souls to enable us to create, experience, and fulfill our unique purpose on this physical plane. To not manifest one's personal destiny is to suffer. *Beyond Belief* relieves suffering by connecting people to The Field and empowering their own unique personal expression and manifestation. One-by-one, as individuals connect and come from this deeper place, humanity is uplifted as a whole and further enabled to reduce suffering and produce ideal outcomes for all.

Ultimately, the mission of **Beyond Belief** is to shift the place from which people are coming: from a place of separation and fear, to a place of connection and love.

"There has been a great and ordered classification and mechanisation, a great discovery and practical result of increasing knowledge, but only on the physical surface of things. Vast abysses of Truth lie below in which are concealed the real springs, the mysterious powers and secretly decisive influences of existence." Sri Aurobindo

Visit www.GoBeyondBelief.com for information on products and services available through Beyond Belief. LLC

2. A TruthBubble for "just what the heck is going on here?" - Evolutionary Panentheism

I know it sounds complicated, but it's actually very simple. Evolutionary Panentheism itself is a product of evolution; it is the current culmination of various very powerful ideas building on one another over time as humanity has explored its world, experience, and place in the universe.

It starts with Theism – the idea that there is a god, outside and above us, that we have fallen from, that the world has fallen from, that we are separate from. You could generically label this as "the god in the sky."

Theism then evolves to Pantheism – when people said, no, god is not outside, separate and above us, god is everywhere and in all things, including us! God is right here! Consistent with this understanding, Sri Aurobindo said, "Apparent nature is secret god."

Pantheism then evolves to Panentheism – when people said, wait a minute, it's BOTH! God is both everywhere, in and through all things (imminent), *and* above, beyond, and outside us (transcendent).

Panentheism has now most recently arrived at *Evolutionary* Panentheism – as people have come to realize the evolutionary nature of our lives, of the earth, of the Universe, and have now applied that "transformation over time" to God itself. That "God is waking up in time," that the current incarnation of the Universe is the current body of God, and is, and has been from the very beginning, becoming and expressing more and more of its inherent Divine Nature. The latent divinity in all things, including us, is waking up and being realized more and more over time.

A good daily practice (like Integral Transformative Practice®) will align us and partner us with the divinity that is both inside us and beyond us. It will accelerate its evolution, and its realization and expression, into our lives and the world. Through a good daily practice, we become more and more Divine, or God-like: more loving, more trusting, more inspiring, more caring, more compassionate, more joyful, more energized, more creative, more capable, more fulfilled…whatever quality you might assign to the Divine is available to us through this kind of a good daily practice. Pretty cool, right?

3. A TruthBubble for Earth - A Positive World Vision

The presence of humanity has fully shifted and is now completely based in love, trust, natural abundance, sharing, openness, listening, and co-creative collaborative partnerships. We have realized that the competition exhibited in our past was unconsciously based in scarcity and fear. With scarcity replaced by abundance and plenty for all, and fear replaced by trust and love, true collaboration and partnership has emerged. The focus now is on serving others, the planet, and the whole, versus getting something to ensure survival.

The human family has moved beyond survival into an experience of abundance. Our historical need to control resources, control people, and control anything is gone. We are now operating in line with universal principles of abundance and love. Coming from this place of knowing, people are open, receptive, and generous. Knowing there is enough for all, the focus of daily activity has shifted to creating through truly collaborative, loving, trusting, partnerships. Nobody *needs* anything since everything is already sourced and provided from within, hence there is a freedom to work with others, unattached, that previously did not exist.

The historical need for police, military, and government to enforce compliance with rules has been drastically reduced. The principle that "Any act of aggression is a cry for help and call for love" is embedded into the culture. For those that have lost their way, people reach out from a place of compassion, offering love, acceptance and support to help restore their alignment with their true source of life. If someone believes they must rob, steal, or hurt anyone to get something, we know they are disconnected from the source of all abundance and therefore we support their authentic re-alignment. The need for violence is gone, and everyone knows that love is the most powerful force in the Universe.

These principles permeate all aspects of life, all walks of life, all endeavors. Up to now fear has been the primary root of creation, hence under all previously created systems was a root of fear. This was seen in the need for control, the belief in lack and scarcity, and the competitive drive to beat and dominate others to survive. With the shift to love as the root, and abundance as the truth, *everything* has shifted.

All systems, processes, and endeavors are now looked at through the lens of love, abundance, and trust and have been completely recreated. Take for example education. Rather than putting in knowledge so a person can get a job, make money, and survive in the world, the first priority of education is to establish the capability of each and every person to connect with their own experience and source of abundance.

This capacity to connect to one's *own* source of life, becomes the primary and fundamental teaching and principle upon which all other education is based; that you already have all the love, all the goods, all the safety, all the happiness right inside you, already given. You do not need to get anything from anybody or anyplace. From this place of knowing abundance, one is truly free to create; to create not from a place of lack and need and fear and survival, but from a place of love, and contribution, and service, and true inspiration aligned with what one's life is all about.

With a solid capacity to connect to their Source of Life established, education then supports and serves each person's highest and greatest calling, their Soul's Purpose, on the planet at this time. And it never ends, education is a lifelong path of growth and discovery. Systems are in place to enable people to learn and grow and constantly be creative on their true life's path of fulfillment, service, and contribution, as it changes over their lifetime.

Coming from Source, there is a knowing that everything is connected – there is nothing that is not me. Every human now knows that harming anything is harming everything, including myself. Integrity is either in or it is out. Humanity is now aware of integrity to the whole knowing that if anyone is suffering, everyone is suffering. With this awareness, human existence becomes life generating and self-sustaining. It integrates seamlessly into the Universe. Just as nature has done, humans now do; all creations arise from the wholistic-system-of-life, live sustainably in that system, and seamlessly return to the system completely and totally serving the emergence of new creations to come. A process that's been known in the past as "Cradle to Cradle" has become a reality for all things. Waste and garbage is a thing of the past. *All* things arise with purpose and *all* things return to the system and serve as a source for new creations. Zero waste is the reality.

Humans are seamlessly integrated into nature, into the Earth's natural, self-sustaining systems. No longer a burden on the planet, we are co-creators of the system itself. Anything that was a "tax" on the system has been recreated to ensure complete and total synergy with the system so that all life is supported and nourished. The re-generative nature of the planet is nurtured and supported. By mimicking nature's process for movement on the planet, we have eliminated all toxic by-products and fully integrated our transportation and movement from one place to another into existing natural systems.

One of the key breakthroughs that has become a reality is free energy – energy that costs nothing, is available to everyone, is unlimited in supply, and is completely integrated into the self-sustaining regenerative natural processes of the planet, indeed of the Universe itself.

Food production has moved in this same direction. The earth is naturally abundant and with transportation now self-sustaining and fully integrated into the planetary system in a free and regenerative form, the whole planet becomes the garden for each and every person. Food supply and distribution is seamlessly integrated into planetary systems and each and every person has an abundance of life giving, supportive, and delicious foods.

Fundamentally what we have created and are experiencing is a Garden of Eden. People, and *all* our activities, are fully integrated into the natural processes of the planet, of the Universe, in a self-sustaining, regenerative manner. Because everyone has everything they need and know that they are the source of that, war is gone, crime is gone, even healing is a thing of the past. When anything goes "awry," the focus is always to restore alignment with Source, with the place from which all things emerge and return to. The planet is a place of amazing beauty, with life abundant in all its forms breath-taking beauty is everywhere.

Space travel is only interesting and needed to the extent Planet Earth is coming to its end of life. Everyone is so happy here on Earth, there is no desire to escape or to find some other place that is better. The only reason to leave is if as a host, the Earth can no longer sustain the life that is here. Even so, we are not attached, knowing that the source of the Universe itself is in all places and that as life, it will emerge in the places in the Universe it is intended to emerge without our having to physically go there.

This is the level of trust in the life force intelligence and energy that exists in and through each and every person. Knowing and experiencing that all needs are always and forever met, we follow our inner expressions for creation. As integral, life generating aspects of the All, moment-to-moment we are co-creating the emerging future and the highest and best for all and everything.

"A perfected community can exist only by the perfection of its individuals, and perfection can come only by the discovery and affirmation in life by each of his own spiritual being and the discovery by all of their spiritual unity and a resultant life unity." Sri Aurobindo

4) A TruthBubble for Death and Dying

While I've always been interested in life after death, and the whole arena of death and dying, after my Stepmother of more than 40 years passed away, and experiencing the impact of that on everyone in my family, I decided to write down my current beliefs, preferences and insights, my TruthBubble, about death and dying. I shared this with many friends and family with the intention of exploring and opening a dialogue on the topic. Death and the afterlife is not something typically discussed, even though its so incredibly important.

This document was my way of distinguishing and sharing where I stand on death and the afterlife, and where I'll be standing as people near and dear to me pass on, since I do extend my TruthBubble into their life and death, regardless of their own TruthBubble on this topic. As much as "their death" is happening "to them," it's happening to me in my life too. And how I hold their death, for me in my life, is my business and is up to me, just like it is for you. I include this here for your own consideration and reflection as you create your own TruthBubble about this incredibly important, and potentially very challenging, area of living: death and dying.

When I Die: Beliefs, Preferences, and Insights
A Celebration of Death (and Life)
Roger K. Marsh, September 2020

Preface

These are MY beliefs, preferences, and insights. I do not need you, nor do I want you, to believe these things because I do. I do not need you to believe these things in order for them to be true for me, just like you do not need me to believe what you believe for those things to be true for you. We are each our own authority; we are each responsible for and creating our own reality and experience in life. So, as you read this, feel free to affirm whatever in here may resonate with you. And at the same time, feel free to reject whatever may not resonate with you. Thank you for honoring my truth as mine and your truth as yours.

Purpose

My purpose in writing and sharing this is multifold: 1) I wanted to get my own thoughts down on paper and organized, as a way of clarifying for myself where I currently stand on this important topic. 2) I hope it can inspire your own reflection and perhaps lead to greater clarity for yourself on this important topic (and if you want to share those things with me I would be happy to hear them). 3) I'm hoping it creates greater willingness to more openly discuss and explore this most fascinating of topics, now, while we are alive. And 4) I hope it can inform those present at my transition to hold and perhaps even witness the transformation and transition that I believe will be happening for me at that time (creating some supportive partners on this side as I journey beyond the body). Thank you!

A Celebration of Death (and Life)

Life is for the living. When I die, I am no longer "here," in physical form, no longer here in the way I had been here up until my passing. I have moved on. Moved on to what's next. Just like I did when I arrived here. I was moving on from what was previous into this life as what was next. Every ending is also a beginning. Every departure is also an arrival. As the boat departs and sails over the horizon and has left the sight of those on this shore, it is arriving and is visible to those on another shore.

It is clear to me that life is a cycle. That things are born, grow and change, and then die, continuously, and forever. You can see this in all things, from the very small cycles to the very large cycles. Each heartbeat dies into the birth of the next one, each breath dies into the birth of the next one, some millions of cells die into the birth of millions of new cells in our body each day, and our entire body, or at least most of it, dies into the birth of a new one approximately every seven years. I am not my body, because if I was, I would, little by little, be gone in seven years. However, "I" persist in existence, what is this that persists in all this physical world change? The body I have today is a totally different one than the body I had seven years ago. Where did my body of seven years ago go and what is it that has remained and stayed?

My death can be a celebration: Roger is free, he has shuffled off the mortal coil (as author and minister Michael Beckwith would say), he's onto what's next and has completed his journey on earth (at least this one), his mission, his duty, his life. I'm sorry I left you behind, however apparently you have more living to do, more lessons to learn, more mission to accomplish, more love to give, more experiences to have before you receive the "green light" to move on.

I believe in reincarnation, in some way, shape, or form. I believe in life after death, I believe there is an aspect of me that continues on beyond this particular body, and takes new shapes and forms, continuing in what I call conscious evolution; developing and expanding consciousness of self and cosmos to greater and greater levels. Why do I believe this? Here's why:

- This is what I have been experiencing in my own life – my own sense of mission and being here to accomplish something beyond the obvious - a soul-based mission coming from a deeper level, a deeper knowing, a deeper nudging and invitation. Who and what I am has been constantly growing and changing ever since I got here. Since I am not my body, why would that stop when the body stops?

- I have read the work of Ian Stephenson (see Wikipedia entry) who has researched and presented 3,000 cases of people having lived previous lives with data so compelling the simplest most obvious answer is reincarnation.

- I have read compelling cases of Near Death Experiences (see here for my favorite one: Anita Moorjani) – there are thousands upon thousands of examples where a person's body and brain is clinically dead, yet they are alive in consciousness and aware of things both near and far, both in this world and beyond, awareness that goes beyond physical capacities even if the person were alive!

- And, because of this additional evidence that supports life beyond this life:

  - Parents will tell you each child has their own personality when they arrive – why is that? What is the source of these unique traits already present in a person before they have had any social conditioning in the world? And along with those traits, some have extraordinary capabilities not developed in this life time, so from where or how were those capacities developed?

  - Astral Body projection and travel – thousands of people report Out of Body experiences or OBEs (see Wikipedia entry) – what goes "out of body" and has these experiences? What sees the body on the bed, or lying on the ground, or anywhere? Something has separated from the body and is now witnessing it, and sometimes other things in other places that would not be known to the person, from "outside." What is that something, and where is that something, that is witnessing these "physical" forms?

◆ Dreams as real as daytime living – some with valuable life guiding insights - what's the source of these experiences?

◆ Quantum Physics demonstrating we are mostly energy (not physical matter), in fact everything is energy. And energy is neither created nor destroyed, it simply changes form.

◆ Quantum Physics (see Resonance Science Foundation for a free online course on Unified Science) demonstrating a Unified Field, a zero point, a metaphysical, non-physical complement to our physical world. A place I suspect I came from, and go back to, as an organized energetic awareness with an infinite evolutionary purpose.

I hope you can celebrate my death, my transition, my graduation, my evolution, my commencement to what's next! My death is a glorious day, a glorious moment, the gift and culmination of a mission fulfilled, a portion of an infinite journey completed, a path walked to the best of my ability. Truly a happy moment worthy of celebration.

For me, it is possible to both love and honor life AND celebrate and be happy at death. Just because I am looking forward to death and will be happy and joyous at my time of transition, does not mean I am hating life, or miserable in life, or trying to hurry up and get it over with. Life has a purpose, I have a purpose in living, and that purpose must be fulfilled, must be honored, and must even be loved and appreciated. I believe it takes great work to incarnate and hold these forms for the purpose they are held for, and that great work is to be appreciated and honored. So, yes, I love my life, AND I look forward to dying and moving on. By loving and embracing and celebrating death, I am able to more fully love and embrace and celebrate life.

Death is the ultimate adventure for the explorer of consciousness. I came into this world pretty much unconscious – or if I was conscious, I don't remember. However, at death, there is a good chance I can enter into that transition fully conscious. In fact, that is my intention. Open mind, open heart, open will – willingly and consciously embracing what is next as the perfect and right thing for my infinite and evolutionary journey.

I like today's shift from a funeral to a Celebration of Life – I think that is appropriate – that we celebrate the life lived by the person who has passed – however I think it is lopsided, just like most things in our society, we pick one side and avoid the other: the material over the immaterial, the left brain over the right, the mind over the heart and soul, the rational over the intuitive, the positive over the negative, the light over the dark, and life over death. In reality, it's always a both/and, you don't get one without the other. So, for me, I want a Celebration of Life AND Death – to consciously bring death into the celebration and restore it to its rightful place in our consciousness.

Death is nothing to be afraid of. Heck, billions upon billions of people right here on Earth have already done it. If it was such a terrible thing do you think we'd keep coming back? Death is good, death is awesome, death is liberating, death is something to be celebrated. And, yes, so is life.

To get a sense of how valuable and important death is, think of how much of a curse it would be to live forever. Stuck here on earth in human form for eternity. What a nightmare. Generations upon generations come and go, and you're still here. This is far different than being an infinite, eternal being. I believe I am an infinite, eternal being. But unlike one who lives forever as a human, as an infinite, eternal being I change forms, I evolve, and I die and am born anew again, and again, and again. THAT is living to me. And it requires death. It requires the old to die so the new can be born. I am embracing this transformation and celebrating the death of the old as a divine and beautiful doorway for the new to be born. The new "me" on the other side of this me. It's a beautiful thing, death, a valuable process to be honored and celebrated. We need it.

A leaf on a tree is a beautiful metaphor for this cycle of life and death. Each year the leaf buds and opens and serves its purpose collecting sunlight for the tree all summer long. Then, as fall approaches, having lived its life and purpose fully, it literally lets go, surrenders fully, falling and returning to the earth from which it literally came. Serving a new purpose, to enrich and support the life of the tree by providing nutrients into the soil for the roots to receive and transport back up into the tree. A beautiful cycle of life AND death. Of living, and letting go. Of serving fully, then returning to source, and embracing new forms and what's next.

Death makes life possible (see IONS research, film and book by that title). So, if we love life, and death is what makes that possible, then it's only fitting we love, honor, and celebrate death too. I am not gone, I have only changed forms and am moving on to what's next – my ship has sailed over the horizon and what looks like a departure to you, is an arrival for others. Just like when I arrived here – I left somewhere I was, to join you, where I am now. And I'll do this again, and again, and again. Amazing.

Affirmation

Hello death, I welcome you, I embrace you, I celebrate and honor you. And when the time comes for my transition, may I do so consciously, joyfully, and easily, honoring the life I have lived, and fully embracing and serving all that comes next.

Made in the USA
Middletown, DE
29 April 2021